GLASGOW &
THE CLYDE
AT
WAR

PAUL HARRIS

ARCHIVE PUBLICATIONS

First published 1986 by Archive Publications Ltd
27 York Road, Bowdon, Cheshire WA14 3EF

Printed in Great Britain by Netherwood Dalton Ltd.
ISBN 0 948946 03 2 Cased
ISBN 0 948946 02 4 Paper

CONTENTS

ACKNOWLEDGEMENTS

Many people have helped me with information and with picture research for this book. I should particularly like to thank those who gave of their time so generously: Neil Morris for his memories of H Morris & Co during the war and for access to their records; Ian Fleming and Jack Grant for their vivid memories of the war as policeman and fireman respectively; John S Gibson for guiding me through the Scottish Record Office files; Norman Burniston for letting me see and reproduce some of the photographs taken by James Hall of Greenock; Mr William McConnell of Rolls Royce PLC and the Rolls Royce Heritage Trust; Murdo Nicholson at the Science & Technology Collection at the Mitchell Library who allowed me to dust off some of the North British Locomotive Company records; John Clayson at the Museum of Transport; and all the library staffs who attended to my queries with patience at the Imperial War Museum (Photographic Section), Glasgow Room of the Mitchell Library, the People's Palace Museum, Clydebank Library, Watt Memorial Library in Greenock, Edinburgh Central Library, Glasgow District Council Archives Department, Strathclyde Regional Archives and last, but far from least, the Glasgow Herald/Evening Times picture library.

Paul Harris
July 1986

INTRODUCTION

Wartime Glasgow – rather like the city in peacetime – has suffered in most books from being painted as unremittingly grey and dismal. In *Officers and Gentlemen* Evelyn Waugh sees the city as some sort of dreary transit camp:

> Glasgow in November 1940 was not literally a ville lumière. Fog and crowds gave the black-out a peculiar density. Trimmer, on the afternoon of his arrival, went straight from the train to the station hotel. Here too were fog and crowds. All its lofty halls and corridors were heaped with luggage and thronged by transitory soldiers and sailors. There was a thick, shifting mob at the reception office. To everybody the girl at the counter replied: "Reserved rooms only."

In the bar of what is patently the Central Hotel, Trimmer meets the statutory tart-with-a-heart-of-gold but this does not relieve the gloom of the city:

> Full, Dickensian fog enveloped the city. Day and night the streets were full of slow-moving, lighted trams and lorries and hustling coughing people. Sea-gulls emerged and suddenly vanished overhead. The rattle and shuffle and the hooting of motorhorns drowned the warnings of distant ships. Now and then the air-raid sirens rose above all. The hotel was always crowded. Between drinking hours soldiers and sailors slept in the lounges. When the bars opened they awoke to call plaintively for a drink.

In Nicholas Monsarrat's *The Cruel Sea* the crew of HMS *Compass Rose* gather in Glasgow to take delivery of their ship. In a hotel in Sauchiehall Street, Bennett is depicted "withholding his custom from a grim-looking tart he had picked up at the bar . . . she had a face like a ruined skull, white and lined: her tight black skirt strained at its seams, overdoing the candour of the flesh, repellent in its allure."

When they return to Glasgow three years later little seems to have changed:

> On this bleak March morning, the grey town was infinitely drab. Spring must come to Glasgow some time, thought Lockhart, as he made his way down Argyll Street, through the crowds of apathetic shoppers, and the depressed hang-dog men waiting for the pubs to open . . . it had the same dour, unimpressionable aspect, the same futureless air, as he remembered from 1939. Presumably something had happened in the meantime: babies must have been born, love must have been made, money must have been lost and won; but it did not show on the grimy wet pavements, nor in the desolate, half-empty shops . . .

But this is to deny the story of the real Glasgow of the Second World War: a bustling hive of activity, one of the most vital cogs in the whole of the war effort and a place of resilience and determination in the face of attack and austerity. The absolutely vital contribution of Glasgow and the Clyde to ultimate victory in the war has never ever been fully acknowledged and, even at this late stage in the day, the crucial role of the area calls for belated recognition.

The bombing probably springs to most people's minds first. For many, Clydebank is synonymous with the bombing but this is not entirely accurate either. Although the Clydebank bombing was devastating in its concentration, Glasgow itself actually suffered worse – and then there was Greenock, Gourock, Paisley, Dumbarton and Renfrew.

For more than a million US and Canadian servicemen the Clyde was their first view of Europe from the decks of the grey painted troopships *Queen Mary* and *Queen Elizabeth*, and hundreds of thousands more from North America and Australasia steamed in to Gourock and Greenock in the great convoys of troops in the build up for the invasions of North Africa and Europe. Then there were the undercover operations and the vital raids launched and – sometimes – welcomed back to Clyde bases. The crippling of the Tirpitz in Altenfjord, the raid on the Lofoten Islands, the attack and evacuation of Spitzbergen, the building of the Mulberry Harbours, the ferrying of vital gold bullion to North America to pay for the war effort and the refuelling, the ammunitioning and storing of the great capital ships of the British navy. There were also, of course, those great products of the Clyde: the merchantmen, the little ships, the battleships and the aircraft carriers built by the men of the Clyde to service the country's insatiable demand for shipping during the dark days of the Battle of the Atlantic. And then there were, more sadly, the wretched survivors of enemy action in the Atlantic for whom the Clyde was a homecoming of an unexpected and involuntary nature.

The Clyde had known it was to go to war as early as 1936/37 when orders were put in hand at factories and shipyards. For men who had lived through the uncertainties and deprivation of the depression of the Thirties the new work was a Godsend and it was tackled willingly and vigorously. The myth of Munich was not the stuff to divert the workers of the Clyde and war came as no surprise on September 3 1939.

The first tangible evidence of conflict came early to the Clyde and it was a surprise. Within hours of the declaration of war, the SS *Athenia* was sunk in the Atlantic en route to Montreal and within 48 hours Royal Navy ships had started to dump the survivors somewhat unceremoniously on the quayside at Greenock. No precedent had been established for dealing with the plight of such unfortunates and a sense of panic and confusion pervades the letters and memos which winged their way between the Corporation of Greenock and the Scottish Office in Edinburgh. Donald MacLean, Inspector of Poor and Public Assistance, was plainly put out when he was moved to write to the Secretary of State for Scotland: "I do think that the survivors ought to have been retained on board the rescue ships until some indoor accommodation had been provided . . . Having visited the scene and witnessed the awful condition of the survivors I, with the concurrence of the Provost and Town Clerk, immediately secured from a large Drapery firm in the town sufficient new clothing comprising Suits, Dresses, Boots etc. and all manner of underwear both ladies, gents and childrens . . . In addition to that Mr Peter Wright, Motor Hirer, West Blackhall Street, Greenock obtained a plentiful supply of hot tea, buns and other suitable food which was very much appreciated by the survivors." But he turns to the nub of the matter later in his letter: "I am also enclosing herewith copy of Accounts for clothing, boots, etc. supplied to the survivors . . . I was informed by the Officer in charge of HMS *Electra* that these accounts would be met either by the Donaldson Line or the Government. The total amount of the accounts is £738 15s 6d . . . I have to state that provision is being made for an ample supply of various articles of clothing and suitable Hall accommodation, adjacent to the Docks, which will be in readiness should another such unfortunate occurrence take place." Alas, such unfortunate occurrences were to become a regular feature of life in Greenock and Gourock over the next few years as survivors of every imaginable type of vessel were brought in to the Clyde.

Greenock managed, in fairly short order, in this instance to unload most of the hapless survivors on the Lord Provost of Glasgow but considerable confusion existed as to who was to pay and for what. Most had no money at all and, initially, the Donaldson Line was reluctant to accept any responsibility – even for onward transportation! Additional difficulties were caused by passengers – especially a Polish contingent – who refused to leave the Clyde unless a neutral American ship or American escorts were produced. Hardly surprisingly, they did not relish the prospect of being torpedoed again. By the end of September nearly all the survivors had been embarked and the Donaldson Line contributed in October the Sum of £5325 towards the cost of the operation. This early problem did serve to concentrate minds and in December it was agreed that shipowners should share with the Government the cost of paying a month's wages to the survivors of wrecked ships.

The sinking of the *Athenia* also sparked off the Clyde's first spy scare and Patrick Sillitoe, the Chief Constable of Glasgow, instituted an investigation into the activities of one of the passengers, an American from Evanston, Illinois, named Gustav Anderson who was travelling on the ship and who was reported to propound in America the German claim that the British sank the *Athenia*. His report is in a document marked SECRET in a file at the Scottish Record Office.

Anderson apparently travelled widely throughout Europe taking copious notes and photographs and had been known to have previously smuggled films out of Russia. ''He seemed inclined to favour the doctrines of Hitler'' and before joining the *Athenia* he travelled to Scotland and spent time ''continually photographing places to which an ordinary citizen would be debarred access''. He apparently represented to a number of people that he was acting on behalf of the American government. When the *Athenia* called at Liverpool on Saturday September 2 he took photographs of the Liverpool balloon barrage, these pictures being taken surreptitiously through a port-hole at lunchtime when the other passengers were eating. The next day, the Assistant Purser was sitting beside Anderson when the first torpedo struck. ''Anderson was the only person who appeared to realise the significance of the explosion.''

As a neutral, Anderson was, of course, inaccessible to the British authorities but this remarkable and little known episode doubtless provided Glasgow police with a rehearsal for things to come.

Every shipload of survivors deposited at Greenock or Gourock had their tale to tell and wartime Britain was treated to a continuing saga of heroism and adventure as recounted by one batch after another of survivors ''landed at a Northern port''.

There was the determination of the crew of the *Imperial Transport*, sliced in two by a torpedo but piloted home with her stern half only afloat, beached on Bute and then rebuilt by a Clyde shipyard to sail again. Then there was the *San Demetrio*, an oil tanker abandoned ablaze by her crew in the Atlantic but reboarded while still white hot and brought home to the Clyde. The tragedy of the evacuee ships taking children to safety in North America was especially bitter. The bewildered children from the *City of Simla*; the courage of the young survivors of the *Volendam* who were met in Greenock at the beginning of September 1940 by

Geoffrey Shakespeare, the Chairman of the Childrens' Overseas Reception Board, and asked if they wanted to try and cross the Atlantic again. ''Yes!'' they said and set off again in the ill-fated *City of Benares* which was torpedoed on September 17 1940, four days out in the Atlantic. Surely a case of 'one woe treading upon another's heel'.

The Clyde saw survivors from the *Empress of Britain*, sunk off the Irish coast by dive bombers and torpedo, of the *Lancastria*, sunk off St Nazaire in the evacuation from France of the summer of 1940 with the highest casualties of any sinking in the War, and the survivors of Hitler's 'unsinkable' battleship *Bismarck*. Of course, it was not all bad news. There was the *Empire Haywood Stanhope*, a merchant ship which sailed from Seville to the Clyde, with a cargo of marmalade and oranges. A German agent operating from Spain had thoughtfully planted delayed action bombs in the crates but when the explosions started en route they were muffled and absorbed by the soft and sticky cargo. When the ship dropped anchor off Hunter's Quay it was decided that all the cases would have to be opened: the oranges were rolled down chutes in bulk into lighters and, you will understand, many dropped into the sea and floated ashore or simply disappeared. Clydesiders enjoyed a feast of rare fruit and – normally unobtainable – delicious marmalade!

The Clyde defences were never breached during the War although the German submarine U-33 attempted to enter the Clyde, under Hitler's direct orders, in February 1940. But three miles off the Pladda Lighthouse the minesweeper HMS *Gleaner* picked up hydrophone noises from the submarine. Successfully attacked with depth charges, the sub was forced to surface, was abandoned and scuttled. No submarine every tried again and the boom across the Tail o' the Bank between the Cloch Lighthouse and the Gantock Rocks by Dunoon was never pierced. For almost two years this was the only narrow entrance to Britain for the gathering invasion forces from America and the Commonwealth. The Thames Estuary was mined. The Bristol Channel was mined. The Mersey was repeatedly bombed. And the North Sea and the east coast were constantly menaced by E boats, U boats and the Luftwaffe. In Britain's darkest hour the Clyde saved Britain.

A Clyde Anchorages Emergency Port Scheme was put into operation shortly after the air attacks on London in September 1940. Stevedoring units from London were billeted in Greenock (some 600 men) and staff were loaned from the Port of London Authority. Within the safely enclosed waters of the Clyde was created a vast port where oceangoing shipping could anchor and, without touching land, load and discharge their cargoes overside.

Thames barges were despatched to the Clyde – either towed around the coasts or carried on the decks of freighters. A fleet of punts was taken to Scotland by road and, under the guidance of a lighterage foreman from London, local Greenock men were trained in the art of handling these craft. All kinds of cargoes were unloaded: bulk grain via portable bucket elevators, large tonnages of explosives and vast numbers of tanks and landing craft in sections, with the help of a powerful floating crane.

There were tricky situations to deal with which would have tested the facilities of a normal port: the restowing of deck cargoes which had shifted in the violent weather of the Atlantic or on the northern route to Murmansk and ships which, severely damaged by enemy action, were so flooded and waterlogged that they arrived with too deep a draught to dock for repairs.

Then there were the great liners: the *Queen Mary, Queen Elizabeth, Aquitania, Ile de France* and *Nieuw Amsterdam* which were regular visitors, their decks packed with troops. These fast vessels travelled singly (no escort could keep up with them across the Atlantic) and upon arrival were unloaded by relays of tenders. It was as tenders that the faithful old Clyde steamers were pressed into service. At the very beginning of the war the Ministry of War Transport had requisitioned the turbine driven *Duchess of Hamilton, Duchess of Montrose, Glen Sannox* and *King Edward*. The paddle steamers were generally converted into flak ships or minesweepers and played a prominent role in the Dunkirk evacuation. The *Waverley* was sunk by a bomb in her engine room, the *Mercury* was sunk by an acoustic mine and *Eagle III* came under heavy fire after running aground. Other actions of the war saw the end of the *Juno* (damaged by a landmine in London Docks), *Marmion* (sunk by a dive bomber off Harwich) and *Kylemore*, lost off the east coast in 1941. Curiously, many paddle steamers from the south of England worked in the Clyde during the war, because of requirements of capacity and draught, and the cross Channel steamer *Maid of Orleans* was a familiar sight in the estuary as she carried American troops from the big troopships. She was later converted in a Glasgow shipyard for Combined Operations duties and was eventually sunk by a mine returning from Arromanches.

It was from the Clyde that a large part of the fleet engaged in the North Africa landings embarked. From here, also, they sailed in large numbers for Normandy, following D-Day, with equipment necessary for exploiting the invasion. In all, from September 1940 to its discontinuance at the end of August 1945, the Clyde Emergency Port discharged and loaded 1,885 ships. The cargo discharged and loaded amounted to 2,056,833 tons while military equipment, stores, mails and other packages numbered more than 6 million.

By far the most potent symbols of all this remarkable effort were the two Queens, painted in coats of sombre grey. In February 1940 only a few hundred people noticed as the *Queen Elizabeth* stole away down the Clyde in secrecy bound for New York. A far different state of affairs than when tens of thousands of people had gathered just four years earlier to see the *Queen Mary* off on her maiden voyage. It was in the Spring of 1942 that the two ships really came into their own with the need to build up troops for the invasion of Europe. The first contingent of US troops – numbering 9,880 – embarked at Pier 90 in New York on the night of May 10. The *Queen Mary* crossed the Atlantic at high speed and in zigzag pattern. She crossed to Gourock in five days, three hours at an average speed of 25.5 knots. Not for nothing the two Queens became known as the 'grey ghosts', arriving and sailing under cloak of darkness with lights extinguished. Routes were constantly changed from as far south as the Azores to as far north as Iceland, signal code books were changed regularly and high speed was invariably maintained.

Often as many as 15,000 troops were carried and the shopping list for the voyage was staggering: 124,300lb of potatoes, 53,600lb of butter, eggs and powdered milk, 31,000lb of sugar, tea and coffee, 29,000lb of fresh fruit, 31,000lb of canned fruit, 18,000lb of jam, 4,600lb of cheese, 155,000lb of meat and poultry, 21,500lb of ham and bacon, 76,000lb of flour and cereals. The logistic operation was daunting and everything on board was literally 'done by numbers'.

Many troops scheduled for embarkation on these two great ships received special training at Camp Kilmer in New Jersey.

Huge wooden mock-ups of the ships were created, including gangways, and the troops practised the boarding process. These operations were filmed and then showed to the troops to point out mistakes and improvements which might be made.

For most Americans arrival in the Clyde afforded them their first view of Britain. The impressions of Ralph Carver, now of New Jersey, are recorded in *Transatlantic Liners at War*:

"We arrived in the Firth of Clyde on October 22 1944 and dropped anchor off Gourock at 0730 hours. We had to remain in our quarters but the crew opened the large doors in the side of the hull. It was from these that we would disembark. Later, I can recall observing the countryside through the doors and being absolutely tantalised by the beauty of the place and the contrast of this port as compared to the port of New York. It was much like being anchored in the middle of the country on the largest ship in the world . . . I remember the very vivid colours. The early morning light, the patches of blue sky and the rays of sunshine coming down through the grey, low hanging clouds. The clouds cast shadows over the various shades of blue, green and grey of the surrounding hills and waters. There were pretty towns in the distance. It was all like a picture postcard."

There were also the celebrities carried during the war years: Fred Astaire, Bob Hope, Sir Thomas Beecham, Bing Crosby, Douglas Fairbanks, Mickey Rooney and many others. And then, of course, there was Winston Churchill.

The *Queen Mary* sailed with him and his party aboard on August 5 1943. Churchill and his retinue were disembarked at Halifax, their destination being Quebec City and a conference with Roosevelt. In all four crossings were made in the *Queen Mary* by Churchill and his party.

In the run up to D-Day, between February and July of 1944, the Queen Mary made six crossing to Britain delivering 75,504 troops. (The total for both ships during 1943 had been 320,500 troops). We all know, of course, of the eventual outcome of the transport of more than one and a quarter million men by the two Queens. On June 15 1945 the tide started to run the other way when the *Queen Mary* took the first US units back home from Gourock.

The writer Paul Gallico graphically summed up the *Queen Mary's* achievements:

"I remember her dazzling speed through the submarine zones, and the graceful and easy way she would lean over into the zigzags to frustrate the undersea wolf packs. I remember her for the way she swallowed up 15,000 GIs at a clip, housed and fed and transported them with never a slip . . . and for the wonderful teeming life that filled her during those war crossings, the ceaseless barking of the loudspeakers".

The final reckoning for the Clyde speaks for itself. A total of 52 million tons of merchandise passed through the Clyde with 2.1 million troops embarked and 2.4 million disembarked. Verily a case of very many owing a great deal to the efforts of relatively few.

For the civilian population the declaration of war meant the opening up of an enormous chasm of uncertainty. It had long been assumed that a new war would be marked by massive and totally devastating air offensives. A few years previously Stanley Baldwin had sagely advised the nation, ''The bomber will always get through'', and this pessimism was itself a product of the limited exposure to aerial bombardment in World War 1.

In June 1917, 17 German planes had dropped about two tons of bombs on Central London, killing 162 people in the area of Liverpool Street Station. This was the worst single incident although in the whole of 1917-18 1,413 civilians were killed by enemy aerial action – which was then still very much in its infancy as a science.

In the run up to the Second War the Government feared that it would be quite unable to cope with the civilian casualties and a Cabinet Committee opined that 5% of all property in the country would be destroyed in the first three weeks of hostilities and so mass evacuation – an organised mass exodus before the event – was seen as a vital preventive measure. The fears of those in Government were communicated clearly to the public and when the warnings were sounded throughout Britain on September 3 there was general fear.

George Beardmore writes in *Civilians at War:*

> It would be impossible to convey the sense of utter panic with which we heard the first Air Raid warning, ten minutes after the outbreak of war. We had all taken THE SHAPE OF THINGS TO COME too much to heart, also the dire prophecies of scientists, journalists, and even politicians of the devastation and disease that would follow the first air raid.

The threat of war from the air did not seem quite so immediate to Clydesiders. A survey carried out at the beginning of March 1941 – just before the mass air raids – by Tom Harrisson's mass observation unit (who so accurately observed the reactions of ordinary folk throughout Britain to the war) revealed that only 30% of people expected heavy raids, 42% were quite vague or indifferent to the threat and 28% were not expecting any large scale raids at all. This last group advanced an interesting set of theories as to why Clydeside might be spared: ranging from the protection afforded by surrounding mountains, magnetic elements in the hills which would dislocate aero engines, the impossibility of locating the Clyde accurately amongst the myriad of west coast lochs, the region was too far from German bases and the attitude – which was especially popular with the upper and middle class respondents – that the Germans believed that revolution would develop on Clydeside so long as the people weren't stirred up by bombs.

Doubtless this last view had its origin in the tardiness with which Clydebank particularly had complied with the national Government's programme of civil defence provision. Supported by the burgh's MP, David Kirkwood, a true 'Red Clydesider', the Labour controlled council had resisted Government pressure arguing that compliance with their edicts was tantamount to accepting the inevitability of war. In a pre-election speech in October 1935 Kirkwood had stated his position unequivocally: ''I am all out for peace in the real sense and would not send a Clydebank boy to war upon any consideration. No war for me under any circumstances.'' This view was obviously shared by his party leader, George Lansbury, when he addressed the Labour Party conference in the same month: ''Those who take to the sword shall perish by the sword.'' This strong current of pacifism pervaded the civic leaders of Clydebank and it was only the compulsory powers under the Air Raid Precaution Act of 1937 which induced them to co-operate.

In reality, of course, Clydesiders were no more 'red' than Londoners were solidly 'blue' and when Churchill departed from an open air meeting in Glasgow at the end of June 1940, massed Glaswegians broke into a spontaneous chorus of ''Will Ye No Come Back Again?'' Angus Calder takes the view in *The People's War* that ''class warfare in the shipyards and factories continued much on peacetime lines.'' But there was, he notes, ''in March 1941 much grumbling about wartime inconveniences which in the south were now taken for granted.''

In many ways the Clyde was better prepared than the English cities had been. There had been time to prepare. Glasgow had benefitted from an energetic Lord Provost in Pat Dollan, there was excellent liaison between departments, emergency feeding plans had been completed, 102 Rest Centres had been set up and there were elaborate plans in hand to move the people on from rest centres to billets to guard against the dangers of disorganised and undisciplined 'trekking', mass evacuations on foot which smacked too much of retreat in the face of the enemy.

At the beginning of March 1941 the town of Clydebank was a 47,000-strong shipbuilding-based community. There was a substantial and well trained complement of both full time and part time civil defence personnel and there was certainly no lack of commitment in this area when the first bombs fell on the night of March 13. The problem was more that over 90% of the children who had been evacuated in 1939 were now back with their families in the town's 12,000 crowded and crumbling tenements. The effects of the two nights raids on Clydebank were devastating. Out of the stock of 12,000 houses, only seven were left undamaged. The nocturnal population (i.e. those actually living in the town) dropped from almost 50,000 to just 2,000 overnight. R H Titmuss chronicled after the war the enormous range and scope of assistance which was required to restore civil life to places like Clydebank: mobile canteens, water carts, ambulances, transport vehicles, doctors, engineers, billeting officers, building workers, building materials, loud-speaker information vans, blankets, medical supplies – the list is seemingly endless.

In Clydebank, more than a third of the housing stock had to be demolished, thus completing Goering's job for him and it was many months before the population could move back in anything like large numbers: 35,000 of the population were left without homes. For about a year and a half 800 workers were engaged full time on repairing houses. In those circumstances it is quite extraordinary to find that virtually all the workers at the shipyards were back to work within 10-14 days, many of them billeted as far as 30 miles away. But after the raids the town emptied as a place to inhabit. Titmuss, a social historian, drily observes: "Where they went to no one knew." Many, in fact, simply took to the hills, camping on the moors above Clydebank.

The tragedy and heroism of these raids has now passed into the realm of local folklore. The bald facts speak for themselves. A total of 439 bombers attacked on two successive nights. More than 1,200 people were killed – 528 in Clydebank – and over 1,100 were seriously injured. On the first night about 270 tons of bombs and 1650 incendiary containers were dropped.

The first wave of bombers arrived over the town shortly after 9.30 in the evening, dropping fairly small bombs with the object of driving people below ground before the second wave dropped the incendiaries. Then, with the area well lit, the heavy bombs would follow. It was a 'bomber's moon': a beautiful clear night with a perfect view, even from 12,000 feet, of the river and all the principal landmarks. Unfortunately, two of the first fires started involved highly flammable material at Singer's timber yard and Yoker Distillery, just over the boundary with Glasgow. (Firefighters still recall the aroma of whisky in the air well into the early hours of the next morning). Other serious fires started in John Brown's shipyard, at the Royal Ordnance Factory, Dalmuir, and in three of the Admiralty oil tanks at Dalnottar. One of these tanks was still ablaze the following night and guided the bombers in – and they promptly set light to another eight.

The attack was virtually unopposed. The anti-aircraft artillery, according to the Brigadier commanding, was as effective as "shooting at a blue bottle in the dark with an air pistol". Two planes were, in fact, brought down – one by a nightfighter in the west

of Scotland and another en route to Clydebank was shot down off the Northumberland coast. The most impressive show of defensive force seems to have been put up by a Polish destroyer which was in John Brown's for repair. Its Ack Ack guns put up a tremendous barrage and reportedly the ship's magazines were completely emptied.

There is an apocryphal story, still recounted to this day, in which it is averred that the Polish guns did shoot down a German plane. The pilot escaped by parachute but by misjudgement or plain ill luck landed on the deck of the Polish destroyer, the Poles seized him and he was immediately despatched by the device of throwing him into the ship's furnace.

Although the defensive barrages may have failed to actually bring any planes down there can be little doubt that their intensity served to shorten the time the bombers spent over the area and damage was accordingly mitigated. When the planes had departed it was time for the firemen, rescue and first aid workers to go into action.

It has been alleged that firewatching was poor and that fires had caught and spread largely without effort at control but things were better organised in the aftermath, despite some serious problems. The largest of the water mains was damaged early in the bombing and the others worked erratically. The local fire brigade coped manfully but when the regional Fire Brigade Inspector arrived from Edinburgh around 4am he authorised the drafting in of units from all over Central Scotland and, indeed, from further afield. On the second night of the blitz Jack Grant, who had joined the AFS in 1938, was drafted in from Edinburgh and he vividly remembers arriving in Clydebank: "There were

Ian Fleming with oil painting 'Bomb Crater, Knightswood', 1942

streets with tenements burning on both sides – even as a fireman I had never seen anything like it . . . it was chaotic."

At that point much confusion was caused by the lack of uniformity or standardisation in hose couplings. Many of the fire brigades drafted in from other parts of the country could not use their own hose for extensions or were even unable to attach them to hydrants. Fortuitously, the Forth and Clyde Canal was near to the blaze at Singer's timber yard and some of the other big fires and firemen were able to draw from it using suction pumps.

Most of those who died in Clydebank died on the first night of blitz: out of the 528 lost it is reckoned that less than 50 died on the second night. The strategem of taking to the hills largely worked although it was not one in which the authorities officially concurred.

The truly extraordinary result of the Clydebank raids was that, from the German tactical point of view, they were an utter failure. Whilst an awful lot of damage was caused and many lives lost, the shipyards were not put out of action, the Rolls Royce Works at Hillington (one of the major targets) was never hit and civilian resolve was actually strengthened. Before the raids there had been a strike of apprentices at John Brown's but within days of the assault they were back at work.

The simple inconveniences were enormous with thousands of workers billeted outside the town and travelling in to work. People slept on the floors in schools and Masonic Halls, in wooden huts and in tents. For the workers who travelled in to work (more than 70% were doing so within 14 days of the raids) water was brought in barrels from Glasgow, two tons of candles and 6,000 boxes of matches were sent to the town and, initially, everybody was dependent upon mobile canteens for food. Everybody available was drafted in to prepare and serve meals from the WVS to the Boys' Brigade and a team of domestic science teachers from Glasgow provided breakfasts for 1,000 and dinners for up to 6,000. There was no shortage of food and, indeed, the meals at the Town Hall were remembered by many as veritable feasts compared with their normal rations, "The one bright spot in our lives – food galore and as much sugar as you wanted!"

Titmuss put forward an interesting view on the remarkably phlegmatic response of Clydebank to the raids when he wrote after the war: "Many of these people had never known the standards of home life, of space, quietness and stability which other people accepted as a matter of course. They looked out on a world of disorder and instability with different eyes, for had they not grown up with hardship by their side during many years of unemployment? To them leaking roofs, broken windows, no schools and a nightly trek to the open fields in springtime meant less than the loss of a job." Thirty years later social scientists were to have a new phrase for this phenomenon – the North-South divide.

Despite the amazing resilience of the population there was a distressing tardiness on the part of some employers to contribute to the efforts of their workers. Initially, workers at John Brown's, for example, could not obtain hot meals at work. The rumblings of this reached as far as the Cabinet in London who learned that John Brown & Co. were reluctant to provide canteens unless the Treasury agreed to the charging of the cost as a revenue expense! In April 1941 Winston Churchill was obliged to write to the company on the subject and meals were provided promptly thereafter.

By April 1 production at Browns was normal. At Beardmores all was normal by the middle of the month. At Singer's war production was up to 50% of its normal level by mid April and the Royal Ordnance Factory was returning to normal production. The story was the same at Turner's Asbestos, D & J Tullis, Clyde Blowers, Dawson Downie and Brockhouse's. Alone of all the major industrial concerns, Strathclyde Hosiery's production had not been resumed, their building having been totally destroyed. Hardly any sort of victory for the Luftwaffe.

The raids of May 1941 were the last great air offensives against the Clyde and this time it was the turn of Greenock and Gourock and Dumbarton. There were some important targets: the Torpedo Factory at Greenock and another one in the old Argyll Motor Works at Alexandria near Dumbarton. Then there was the Blackburn Aircraft Factory at Dumbarton where the Sunderland Flying Boat was manufactured. Dumbarton and Greenock were well prepared with decoy strategies although these worked better for the first named town.

A dummy town had been built on the hills above Dumbarton out of canvas and wood and where even the lighting was similar to the actual town. When the first wave of planes came over Dumbarton on the night of May 5 as usual they dropped incendiary bombs to guide the next wave in. These fires were rapidly doused and then decoy fires were set off in the dummy township high on the hill.

There was soon a massive fire burning on the moors and as a result most of the bombs dropped were dropped on the moors rather than in the actual town: after the raid 90 craters were found on the moors and it was estimated that only 20 bombs were dropped on the town itself. There were only 18 lives lost in Dumbarton.

Things did not work out so well though across the river in Greenock where 280 people were killed and more than 1000 homes destroyed. There was a small raid on the night of May 6 on Greenock but it was the next night that there came the real baptism of fire. More than two hundred planes attacked the town in three waves: the first with incendiary bombs to light the way for those following and which, unfortunately, set light to the distillery in Ingleston Street; the second with incendiaries and high explosive bombs and the third wave, around 2am, with parachute landmines and high explosive bombs. The distillery blaze was not doused and it lit the way for subsesquent waves. "The whole area of the town between James Watt Dock and Cathcart Street seemed to be ablaze," according to John Liddell, Deputy Town Clerk at the time. Nearly 10,000 houses out of the stock of 18,000 were damaged and around 1,000 were totally destroyed. Walker's and Westburn sugar refineries received direct hits, Lamont's drydock was put out of action, the distillery on Ingleston Street was destroyed, Dellingburn power station was put out of action and much of Cathcart Square was destroyed. The work of regeneration was to take a very long time but John Liddell's words could have applied equally to any part of Clydeside: "It took many months and, indeed, years to repair and replace most of the damage, but the resilience of the civilian population caused the corporate life of the community to make a remarkable recovery. Despite extreme inconvenience and almost insuperable difficulties, industrial production was rapidly resumed in a spirit of comradeship and endeavour . . ."

And as another survivor put it, "Morale was better in Greenock after the blitz than before it . . . people really came together."

It is really quite surprising how few photographs of life in Glasgow and on the Clyde during the Second War have survived. Of course, fewer people had cameras which were not, anyway, the nifty pocket items of today. For servicemen the possession of a camera on duty was a serious offence and although some managed one way or another to keep a camera, photographic materials were, in any case, difficult to come by and there was the problem of processing.

Such was the fear of fifth columnists that the very act of taking a photograph – let alone taking it to be processed – would often provoke swift reaction. One of the few authorised photographers on the Clyde was James ('Jimmy') Hall of Greenock, some of whose photographs are reproduced here. He undertook many top secret assignments for the Royal Navy and was later granted the commission of Lieutenant, R.N.V.R. (Special Branch). Very often even he was not allowed to process his own plates of the tests on some new underwater device or other. Instead they were taken direct to the Admiralty by courier where they probably still lie today. He photographed the troop convoys, the effects of the bombing and the survivors from the sea as they stepped ashore at Gourock and Greenock. The story is told of his attempt to photograph Winston Churchill, then First Lord of the Admiralty, when he visited the Clyde in February 1940 to visit the officers and men of the damaged Home Fleet flagship HMS Nelson, mined off Lock Ewe.

"Put down that camera," barked Churchill, surprised to see the photographer.

Later, relenting, he allowed his photograph to be taken and Jimmy Hall proffered Churchill the print of a photograph taken only the day before of the Queen Elizabeth leaving the Clyde in secrecy for the very first time. Churchill stared at the picture, taking in the majestic sight of the great Queen in the Clyde.

"That goes in my personal album," he said. "It makes up for this," and he waved towards the crippled battleship in the river. "It makes the trip north well worthwhile."

On another occasion the glint of a camera lens was espied by a sharp eyed naval officer on the bridge of his ship in the Clyde. A full scale spy alert was sounded and a hastily convened shore party sped to the area where, of course, they discovered Jimmy Hall taking official photographs for the Navy.

There was no such problem for artist Ian Fleming who, as a Police War Reserve Sergeant in the Maryhill Police 'F' Division, simply stood at the site of incidents, his police notebook out but, instead of the usual dreary notations, he made sketches which, in his moments off, he worked up,''with the aid of a retentive memory'' into etchings at his home in Saxon Road, Knightswood. His series of etchings of Glasgow under fire are unique and powerful statements about war on civilians.

He admits to being influenced by Goya – "his 'Disasters of War' was a bible to me" – and in many

ways they have a passion and reality superior to any photograph. Fortunately, they are now in the possession of the People's Palace Museum in Glasgow.

There are a number of photographs in this book which could not be published at the time. Newspapers could not publish pictures which might undermine morale nor which specifically identified strategically important locations, names of ships and so on. Photographs were submitted to the office of the censor before publication and changes were made to captions and instructions often given for the deletion of parts of the pictures. In the files of the Evening Times and Glasgow Herald one comes across the hand of the censor time and again. "Scottish port" becomes "Northern port" or, even, plain "British port". A picture of child evacuees, in the wake of the sinking of the first 'seavac' ship Volendam, leaving the Clyde is marked on the back as passed for publication by the Press and Censorship Bureau, August 14 1940, with "Scottish port" changed to "Northern port" and "embarking some time ago" added in red to the caption.

It is now known that Germany was never able to successfully place a spy in the Clyde area during the war but, rightly, no chances were taken with the leakage of sensitive information. In the same way, it was only revealed at the end of the war that the cruiser HMS Curaçao, escorting the troopship Queen Mary to the Clyde, had been run down by her charge in the Western Approaches on October 2 1942.

The Curaçao was sliced in two by the great liner and 331 officers and crew from her complement of 432 men perished. The Queen Mary did not even reduce speed but sailed on to the Clyde out of reach of possible attackers. The incident was observed by hundreds of American servicemen aboard the Queen Mary but all were sworn to secrecy and it was June 1945 before the relatives of those who died learned of what happened. In the Clyde, shipwrights boarded the Queen and concrete was poured in to strengthen the bows which now sported a dent above the waterline. Quickly repaired, she resumed her Atlantic shuttle service: John Brown's had made her to last.

Similarly, the Clyde never gave up the secret of the Luftwaffe's lucky direct hit, on the night of September 18 1940, on the cruiser HMS Sussex lying at Yorkhill Basin. About to put to sea on the demanding convoy run to Murmansk, she was put out of action for almost two years at the very time she was most needed. The Luftwaffe pilot, who had released his bomb from the clouds high above the city, flew home without so much as a glimmer of his achievement – but how William Joyce, Lord Haw Haw, would have rejoiced for the news of this coup. Hundreds of local people in the area were evacuated before the 500lb bomb could be defused and many thousands of workers the next day could see the evidence of the pilot's incredible luck as they poured into the city on rush hour trains on the railway bridge over the river. The cruiser was all but a total wreck, split open and keeled over in the river but the enemy did not learn of the incident for many months: the shield of security which surrounded wartime Clydeside kept the secret.

The tracing of photographs of industrial activity during the War raised different problems. Time and again I was told that there were no photographs in the files. "We've been taken over three or four times since the War," was the sad response all too often. It is a tale of lost records, destroyed or shipped south into the maw of some multi-national and lost for ever. One librarian told me the heartbreaking story of arriving at a factory as hundreds of glass plates of war activity were loaded into a skip. But he learned that apparently the gatekeeper had salvaged hundreds of the plates and taken them home. He sped to a comfortable Glasgow suburban bungalow to ask to see the plates. "Surely," obliged the gatekeeper cheerily. "Just come with me and I'll show you all those plates." He led the librarian into his garden and pointed proudly to his new greenhouse. Every plate had been painstakingly cleaned and used in the horticultural construction.

Fortunately, a few family firms who have survived have retained the photographic evidence of their contribution to the war effort and some foresighted enterprises have donated their records to the Scottish Record Office, Mitchell Library or the Imperial War Museum. But they are, alas, relatively few in number and in most instances all the evidence is now gone and can never be brought back. It would be gratifying indeed if, perhaps, the compilation of this small selection of pictures of Glasgow at War drew the attention of holders of material to the value of their collections.

Typical of the paucity of illustrative material dealing with the period is one major Glasgow reference source (and I forbear from naming it lest it be besieged by hunters after the macabre), which has, in total, in its collection just over one dozen photographs plus an extraordinary and hideous book of the dead: photographs taken in temporary mortuaries of the unidentified dead of the massed raids of March 1941, their faces horribly creased and contorted by their terminal experience. Pictures of children who look like old men, women straight from 'Macbeth' – for a graphic representation of the horrors of war you need look no further.

Yet I find it strange that this of all collections of pictures should be the one and only to survive. Could it be indicative of a certain thoroughness approaching the Teutonic or, perhaps, is it simply that there was nothing left to censor in the cold, hard reality of death, that one sure certainty of life? One part of me wanted to reproduce one of these truly terrible pictures here but I closed the large, heavy volume and sent it back to the vaults where it belonged. And the dead to their rest.

In Room 21 on the first floor of the North British Hotel (now the Corpthorne Hotel) in Glasgow's George Square there took place on the evening of Friday January 17 1941 one of the most momentous dinner parties of the whole War: momentous in its implications and an event which determined the whole outcome of the war.

The beginning of 1941 saw Britain at her lowest ebb in the battle against Hitler. She was at bay. Blitzes on the ports, catastrophic losses of merchant shipping and with Nazi troops in unchallenged control of the continent of Europe from North Cape to the Pyrenees, the situation was indeed grim. The morale of the people of Britain was at its lowest point ever and Tom Harrisson's Mass Observation team reported that 40% of the population no longer followed the war news at all. Absenteeism and industrial stoppages were a blight on the war effort. Even coalmen were not delivering the coal. Britain stood alone in the world and it was against this unhappy background that President Roosevelt sent his own special envoy, Harry Lloyd Hopkins, to Britain on January 9 1941 to assess the resolve of the British people in this period of deep crisis and, by implication, the arguments, if any, for supporting the old country.

Just after his arrival he observed to the American Military Attache, General Raymond E Lee, "They must prove that they are doing their best before we go all out for them."

Churchill had lunch with Hopkins on January 10 and invited him to travel north with him to Scapa Flow where Lord Halifax was joining the *King George V* to sail for America to take up his post as British Ambassador. On the way back from a rapid tour of naval bases in the north of Scotland they were met in Edinburgh by Tom Johnston, Secretary of State for Scotland designate, and on January 17 travelled to Glasgow. There was a whirlwind tour of Civil Defence units in the city and then the dinner in what is now named the Hopkins Room. According to John Gibson, in his history of the Scottish Office, the envoy was ominously silent and unimpressed on this closing evening of his Scottish visit. Things did not appear to be going smoothly.

It occurred to William Ballantine, late Director of the Scottish Information Office, to remind Tom Johnston of Hopkins' grandmother's origins in the Perthshire village of Auchterarder. A note was passed to Johnston and the conversation was duly pointed in that suggested direction. The result was dramatic and, quite literally, world shattering.

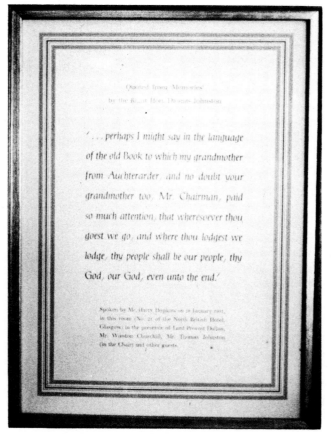

Commemorating Harry Hopkins' historic visit.

Tom Johnston got to his feet: "We have tonight with us a friend from overseas. If he cares to say a word to us we shall be delighted. This is quite an informal gathering. No press representative is present. And more particularly do I welcome Mr Hopkins for the sake of his old grandmother from Auchterarder."

The room was hushed as Harry Hopkins got slowly to his feet. His voice barely more than a whisper, he looked down the table and addressed Churchill directly.

"I suppose you want to know what I am going to say to President Roosevelt upon my return. Well, I'm going to quote you one verse from that Book of Books in the truth of which Mr Johnston's mother and my own Scottish mother was brought up. 'Whither thou goest, I will go; and where thou lodgest I will lodge; thy people shall be my people, and thy God, my God''.

And, his voice cracking, Hopkins added three final words that formed no part of the Book of Ruth: "Even to the end."

Those in the room sat in stunned silence. And then Winston Churchill, Prime Minister of battered and beleagured Britain, broke down and wept unashamedly.

And so it was in Room 21 of the North British Hotel in Glasgow's George Square that the United States of America pledged its support to this country in its fight against Fascism and the whole course of the Second World War was changed.

Four years later, with the undiluted aid of our Commonwealth and American allies, the tide had been well and truly turned and on March 7 1945 the first American troops crossed the Rhine into Germany. Unconditional surrender was but two months away but in Britain people's feelings were light years away from those at the nadir of the country's fortunes in 1941. The attitudes and efforts of people on Clydeside had been little different from those elsewhere in the country but the mantle which had been thrust on their shoulders in those dark days was one of an importance unparallelled in Britain.

It was the Clyde that built the ships. It was the Clyde that succoured and sheltered the vital convoys. It was from the Clyde that the Battle of the Atlantic was fought and won. And it was the Clyde that provided the country's only entry for the hundreds and thousands of troops who were to bring down Nazism. In return – far from alone – the civilian population reaped the harvest of bombs and hardship. But when the rest of Britain needed the Clyde it was not found wanting and the challenge was taken up wholeheartedly by Glaswegians and all Clydesiders.

This is not a definitive history of Glasgow's involvement in the Second World War but an attempt to capture the spirit of the time: may these pages bear witness.

WAR IS DECLARED

1   It's official! The *Evening Times* bill and vendor.

The formal declaration of war on September 3 1939 scarcely came as a surprise. Planning for war had long been in hand. Perhaps the greatest fear was of the widespread damage and loss of life which bombing would cause and during that first weekend in September 170,000 schoolchildren and mothers were ''spirited away'' to the comparative safety of the country and the seaside from Edinburgh, Dundee, Glasgow and Clydebank (8-13). The anticipated onslaught failed to develop and over the winter of 1939-40 an estimated three quarters of the evacuees were to return to their homes in the city. Nevertheless, the actual evacuation was a miracle of organisation.

The impact of war came early to Greenock with the sinking of the SS *Athenia* on September 3 just a few hours after the declaration of war. The Inspector of Poor and Public Assistance wrote to the Secretary of State for Scotland: ''On the morning of Tuesday, 5th instant at 8.15 I received a 'phone message from the Town Clerk informing me that a large number of the survivors of the 'Athenia' had been deposited on the Albert Harbour from HMS 'Electra' and 'Escort' and that the large majority of them were scantily dressed and also required hospital treatment.

''When I tell you that these people were landed at the same pier as where a sugar boat was busily unloading and there being no shelter or lavatory accommodation, you can understand the utter confusion that existed . . .''

The problem presnted by the survivors of the *Athenia* (4, 5) was, of course, a novel one at the beginning of September. Alas, before many months were out it was to become an all too familiar feature of life on the Clyde.

2   Rifle practice at the depot of the 2nd Battalion The Cameronians shortly before war was declared.

3   The pipes and drums of the 2nd Battalion The Cameronians.

4   SS *Athenia* leaves the Clyde on her last voyage shortly before war was declared.

5

Within a few hours of the declaration of war the SS *Athenia* is torpedoed 200 miles west of the Hebrides. The survivors are brought back to the Clyde on September 5.

6   Precautions against expected air raids were quickly instituted. Well known Glasgow drapers Pettigrew & Stephens took precautions against the danger of flying glass.

7   An office of *The Glasgow Herald* and *The Bulletin* is protected with sandbags.

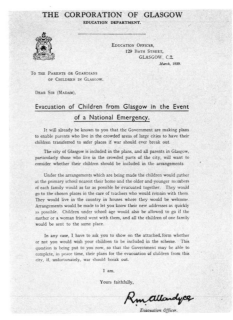

8

Plans for the evacuation of children from the Glasgow area had been put in hand long before the outbreak of war. The evacuation of children started September 1st 1939.

9   Two young evacuees. A little girl is comforted by her sister.

10   There is obviously more adventure in *The Beano* than in the drama of their evacuation for these youngsters!

11

Off to the country — everyone sporting luggage labels for identification.

A train full of evacuees leaves Glasgow September 3.

13   The last bus leaves with evacuees from East Park Home – bound for Largs.

At the end of the first week of the war Glasgow had just one bright spot – this bookshop in West Nile Street with its windows left burning in defiance of blackout regulations.

14

CIVIL DEFENCE

15   Tenants in Culross Street, Sandyhills, try out their new shelter in the back garden after delivery in February 1939.

The establishment of ARP arose out of Cabinet approval in 1935 for the spending of £100,000 on planning for the contingency of war. It was widely expected that aerial bombardment would start within hours, if not minutes, of the outbreak of war. By the end of 1938, 1.4 million people had joined ARP in the wake of the Munich crisis.

Most ARPs were Wardens whose job it was at the beginning of the war to enforce the blackout and then later to judge the extent and type of any damage in their particular area so that the local Control Centre could send appropriate rescue services. The local knowledge of the Wardens was deemed to be vital in getting survivors out as speedily as possible. Once out, it was the further responsibility of the Warden to get survivors to a shelter or a Rest Centre. More than 90% of Wardens were part-timers and around 20% were women.

Under the direction of the Control Centre were First Aid parties and Rescue Men. ARP also embraced the Women's Voluntary Service who manned canteens and Rest Centres.

The most important ARP work was preventative as in evacuation and the use of shelters. Shelters were marketed to the population of Glasgow during the Spring of 1939 with various designs of shelter on display in George Square, Central Station and St Enoch Square (15-17) and they were manufactured extensively by local firms. The Hudson shelter, it was announced, was made from "Dalzo rust-resisting plates and weighing about 13 cwt. . . . the design has been submitted to the Home Office who state that it is suitable for four persons and that 'it will give admirable protection against splinter and blast of high explosive bombs and overhead cover from the incendiary bombs' when properly sandbagged.'' This particular model was advertised at just £30, "supplied in one piece" and thus requiring "no assembling in situ". *The Bulletin* observed, "For houses in which it is not convenient to construct a room to afford the necessary protection without involving expensive structural alterations the shelter appears well suited to providing a good refuge for an average suburban family". Still, not quite the sort of thing for a cosy weekend!

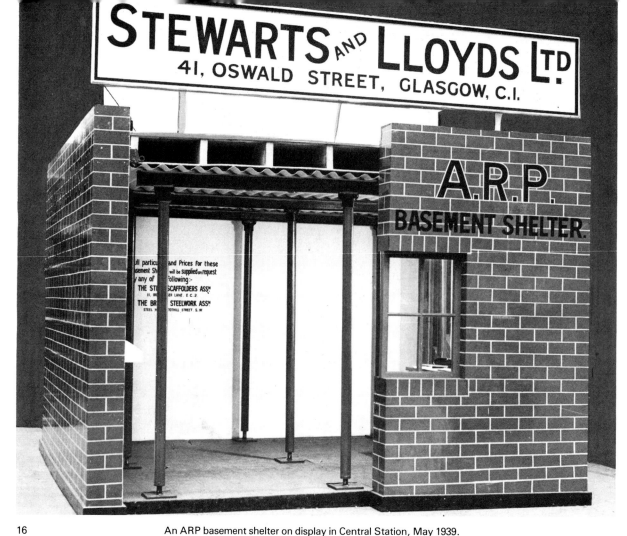

16   An ARP basement shelter on display in Central Station, May 1939.

The Hudson ARP shelter photographed in St Enoch Square, April 1939.

17

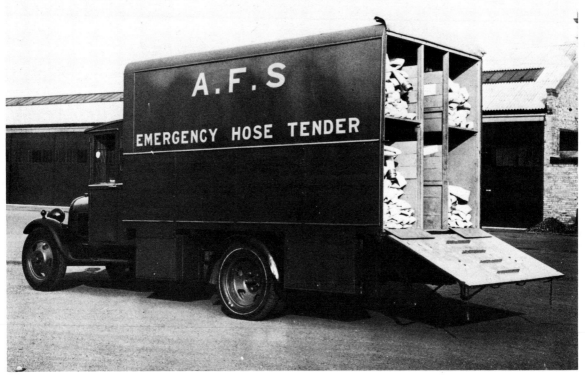

18   AFS Emergency Hose Tender.

Glasgow Fire Brigade
AUXILIARY FIRE SERVICE

SUPPLEMENTARY FIRE PARTIES

In view of the necessity for all citizens of either sex to assist in protecting the City in their IMMEDIATE NEIGHBOURHOOD against incendiary attack, and in so doing to defeat the purpose of such an attack, every person capable of rendering such assistance is requested forthwith to intimate his or her willingness to do so, and to receive such training and instruction as is necessary for the address to :

who will pass on the information to your Ward Committee, in order that you may be enrolled as a member of the Supplementary Fire Parties Scheme which that Committee is organising for your district.

This is a case for ALL hands to the pumps.

M. CHADWICK,
Firemaster.

Fire Brigade Headquarters,
33 Ingram Street, Glasgow,
January, 1941

CORPORATION OF GLASGOW

AIR RAID PRECAUTIONS

DAMAGE TO THE WATER SUPPLY SYSTEM

Prevention of Enteric Fever, Etc.

IF MAINS ARE EXTENSIVELY DAMAGED YOU MUST PURIFY THE WATER YOU USE UNTIL FURTHER NOTICE BY—

(1) BOILING THE WATER ; or

(2) ADDING CHLORINATED-SODA SOLUTION.*

10 drops of chlorinated-soda solution should be added to each pint (2 tumblerfuls) of water, or two teaspoonfuls to each pailful of water. After stirring, the water should stand for 5-10 minutes before use.

* This can be purchased from your local chemist.

19

20

All hands to the pumps! Notice issued by Glasgow Firemaster.   Air Raid Precautions Notice issued by Glasgow Corporation.

21   Corporation of Glasgow ARP Rescue Service truck and trailer.

Interior of a mobile canteen photographed at Larkfield Bus Works.

22

23   Lord Provost Dollan together with other members of the Corporation inspects shelter trenches on Glasgow Green, October 1939.

24   Even the milk supply was camouflaged! The Crow Road milk pasteurisation plant, sandbagged and camouflaged.

25   The main entrance to Glasgow Corporation Transport offices in Bath Street.

26   Firemen tackle a fire in a dummy building during the fire services display in George Square during Glasgow Warships Week, October 1941.

THE HOME GUARD

27   Battle school demonstration by the 1st Glasgow Battalion of the Home Guard, March 1944.

The activities of 'Dad's Army' can now be relied upon to bring a wry smile to the lips but its establishment arose out of very real fears. When the Germans invaded Holland and Belgium in May 1940 their paratroops played a leading role and Britain also feared a parachute invasion. On May 14 when Anthony Eden appealed for men between 17 and 65 to form anti-paratroop units guarding installations like factories, power stations and railways there was a tremendous response. At first the units were mainly groups of employees protecting their own works premises and they were called Local Defence Volunteers.

On September 7 1940 the Home Guard in Glasgow was turned out by the ringing of church bells. This was the prearranged signal to announce the landing of German parachutists. Fortunately, it was all a ghastly mistake but as a no doubt red-faced officer explained, "It proved to be a splendid exercise." And added, in the true traditions of 'Dad's Army', "The mistakes that were made were the result of over-enthusiasm on the part of the men".

28   Dunbartonshire Local Defence Volunteers enlisting May 25 1940.

29   Dunbartonshire LDVs. A picquet, June 1940.

LDV Parade at Bishopriggs, July 1940, held as part of a recruiting campaign.

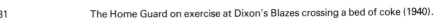

31   The Home Guard on exercise at Dixon's Blazes crossing a bed of coke (1940).

32   Glasgow Home Guard Church Parade. Men pictured entering Ascot Cinema, Anniesland (1941).

33   The Home Guard hold up and question an army officer on a motorcycle (1941).

The perimeter defence of Glasgow entailed setting up machine gun posts around the city. Here gunners prepare to hold an important bridge on Home Guard exercises.

A red letter day for Home Guard men at Newton Mearns when Hitler's deputy, Rudolf Hess, crashed his Messerschmitt 110 and landed by parachute, May 10 1941.

A RIVER AT WAR

A familiar Clyde scene during the War as Allied shipping assembles at the Tail o' The Bank.

By its very definition the Second World War was a global conflict and in all respects it was the most wide ranging war ever fought – which affected every continent and every ocean in an all pervasive way unequalled in any previous conflict. In the context of a worldwide war with associated reliance on supply, transport and communication, the Clyde assumed an importance unparallelled in its history.

Within two days of the declaration of war the first convoy had left the Clyde – in this case for Gibraltar. Throughout the war convoys were to gather at the Tail o' the Bank behind the boom between the Cloch Lighthouse and Dunoon (76) in the secure anchorage offered by the Clyde beyond the reach of U-boats and enemy aircraft. The two Queens – *Queen Mary* and *Queen Elizabeth* – operated a 'shuttle' service between the Clyde and North America transporting more than a million troops in the process. Warships gathered, ran the measured mile, refuelled, victualled and their crews enjoyed the rest and recreation of Glasgow. Our allies sailed in in great convoys and, more sadly, the survivors of the Battle of the Atlantic were, more often than not,

deposited on the Clyde quayside.

It was thus that the Clyde became associated with some of the most epic and heroic dramas of the war. Like the story of the Imperial Transport (38-9) cut in two by a torpedo in February 1940. Captain Smiles and his crew then sailed the stern half of their ship for three days before they were taken in tow and eventually the stricken oil tanker was beached at Kilchattan Bay on the Isle of Bute before being towed up the Clyde for rebuilding!

Then there was the tanker *San Demetrio* (43), attacked in mid-Atlantic by the *Admiral Scheer,* abandoned by her crew ablaze and, to all appearances, sinking. Two days later she was reboarded by her crew – still ablaze and white hot, her bridge and accommodation gutted. Eight days after the surface raider's attack her crew brought the battered ship into the Clyde "by guess and by God", according to Second Officer Hawkins.

The heaviest loss of life at sea in the whole war was caused when enemy dive bombers sank the troopship *Lancastria* (40) off St Nazaire on June 17 1940 during

37   For tens of thousands of survivors of Nazi torpedo and air attacks on shipping the Clyde was their first view of home. Here are pictured the survivors of HMS *Carinthia* torpedoed in June 1940.

the evacuation from France. There were 2,833 lives lost and many of the survivors were brought back to the Clyde.

When U-47, commanded by Captain Prien who sank the *Royal Oak* in Scapa Flow in October 1939, sank the *Arandora Star* off the West coast of Ireland at the beginning of July 1940 her captain and crew did not realise that the liner carried 1,500 German and Italian internees bound for Canada. Of these, 470 Italians and 143 Germans lost their lives and, again, the survivors were brought back to the Clyde (41-2).

Things must have looked bad enough for the hapless children who reached the Clyde, having survived the sinking of the Dutch liner *Volendam* (44) on August 30 1940, but when they were re-shipped from Liverpool two weeks later aboard the *City of Benares* little could they guess that lightning might strike twice.

Seventy-seven children died and forty-six survivors were brought back to the Clyde after an eight day ordeal in a storm-lashed lifeboat in the North Atlantic. In the lifeboat the boys speculated on the possibility of their getting kilts if they were to land up in Scotland. News of

this reached Glasgow Corporation and they were fitted out with kilts on arrival (49) and had tea with the Lord Provost at the City Chambers (48).

The liner *Empress of Britain* had brought tens of thousands of Canadian, Australian and New Zealand troops to Britain by way of the Clyde and those whose journeys had ended safely mourned the sinking of the ship off the Irish coast in October 1940 (50-2).

The Glasgow ship *Kemmendine* was sunk by a raider in the Indian Ocean in July 1940. The survivors were taken to Italian Somaliland as prisoners and liberated the following year when the British invaded. They arrived back in Glasgow more than a year after their departure (53).

Survivors of the sinking of the unsinkable – the German battleship *Bismarck* (55-7) – and refugees from the raids on the Lofoten Islands (67-8) and on Spitzbergen (71-3) all ended up in Scotland via this great artery. And through all this drama and disaster the Clyde launched even more ships which sailed majestically down river (74-8).

38   On February 11 1940 the *Imperial Transport* was cut in two in a torpedo attack in the Atlantic. Her crew sailed the stern half back to the Clyde where she is seen in tow to the shipyard for rebuilding.

39   A Clyde shipyard did the seemingly impossible and repaired the *Imperial Transport* and she returned to sea.

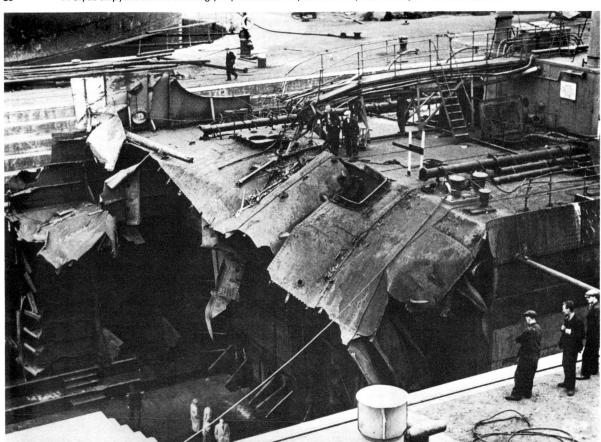

Survivors of the troopship *Lancastria* were brought back to the Clyde after the former Cunard-White Star Liner was sunk off St Nazaire by Junkers dive bombers. In this dramatic picture survivors clamber from a rescue trawler aboard a transport for the Clyde.

40

41

42

On July 2 1940 the *Arandora Star* was torpedoed and sunk by a German submarine in the Atlantic. What the U-boat Captain did not know was that she was transporting 1,500 Italian and German internees to Canada.

Some of the survivors of the *Arandora Star* are landed at Gourock.

The return of the *San Demetrio* to the Clyde after she was attacked on November 5 1940 was an inspiring epic voyage for wartime Britain. Here are most of the crew members who brought the ship back home.

43

44   Evacuee children rescued from the *Volendam* arrive in the Clyde, September 1 1940.

45

Young Robert Wilson, a survivor of the *Volendam*. There were 74 Scottish youngsters aboard out of a total of 320 children.

A group of survivors. Behind is the Eastern Star Canteen gifted by the Order of the Eastern Star in Canada to the AFS in Greenock.

47 Survivors of the ill-fated evacuee ship *City of Benares*, sunk in the Atlantic September 26 1940. Pictured here is 6-year-old Terence Jeffries with some of his schoolmates.

48

City of Benares survivors Louis Walder, John Baker and Rex Thorne photographed at the Municipal Chambers in George Square.

49

Three *City of Benares* survivors fitted out with Highland Dress at Dowans, Buchanan Street.

50

The Canadian Pacific liner *Empress of Britain* was a regular visitor to the Clyde but on October 26 1940 she was attacked and sunk by enemy aircraft off the Irish Coast. Some survivors enjoy a welcome sandwich on arrival in the Clyde.

51

Survivors of the *Empress of Britain*.

52

Rescued crew members arrive at Gourock.

Members of the crew of the Glasgow ship *Kemmendine* photographed on arrival in the Clyde. Captain R B Reid (wearing hat) and included in group are crew members G Gibb, J Park and L Holland.

Captured German merchantmen landed at Gourock.

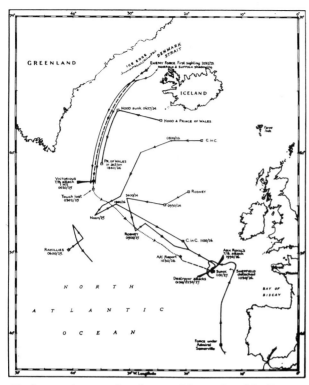

55 The interception, pursuit and eventual destruction of the German battleship *Bismarck* ranged over a vast area of the Atlantic.

56 Survivors of the *Bismarck*, formerly the heaviest and most powerful battleship afloat, come ashore on the Clyde.

57 A wounded German seaman from the *Bismarck* is carried ashore. At the time the censor required the removal of the British officer before the photograph could be published.

58 The *Empress of Britain* in the Clyde June 14 1940. She arrived in the company of the *Aquitania* (seen in the distance), *Empress of Canada* and the *Queen Mary* with the first contingent of Australian and New Zealand troops to arrive in Britain.

59 The Australian troops on the quayside.

Troops of the 28th (Maori) Battalion disembark at Gourock.

60

61

The first Canadian contingent arrives at Greenock at the end of 1939. Pictured here is the officer commanding, Major General McNaughton, Mr Anthony Eden and Mr Massey.

62

Canadian troops come ashore at Greenock.

63   Pictured shortly before she sank on April 30, 1940, the Free French destroyer *Maille Breze* off Greenock.

General de Gaulle visits Free French Forces in Greenock, Christmas Day 1941.

64

65   Evacuee children leave the Clyde for a new life in South Africa.

Prize of war! Nazi blockade runer *Wahehe* was captured as she tried to run the blockade from Vigo but she was taken in the North Atlantic
66   and brought to Kirkwall and then Greenock.

67   Back in the Clyde from the raid on the Lofoten Islands in March 1941 two 'Tommies' display their souvenirs.

68   Soldiers and seamen returned from Lofoten show off the flag of a German armed trawler sunk in the successful raid.

69   Firefighting in Rothesay Docks, September 18 1940.

70   Special firefighting barge at Rothesay Docks.

71   The Spitzbergen raid was launched from the Clyde in September 1941 and the local population brought back to the Clyde for settlement in Scotland. These are some boy scouts pictured after arrival.

A Norwegian Red Cross lady with a young Norwegian boy from Spitzbergen.

Two children from Spitzbergen. The little girl is wearing a reindeer skin coat.

75   Utility aircraft carrier HMS *Archer* at anchor in the Clyde.

74   His Majesty King George VI visits one of his utility aircraft carriers in the Clyde.

76   Aerial view of the boom which protected shipping in the Clyde. The picture is taken from above the Cloch Lighthouse, looking towards Dunoon. Note the guardships and narrow entry in the middle.

Hitler Put a Price on the Two Queens' Heads

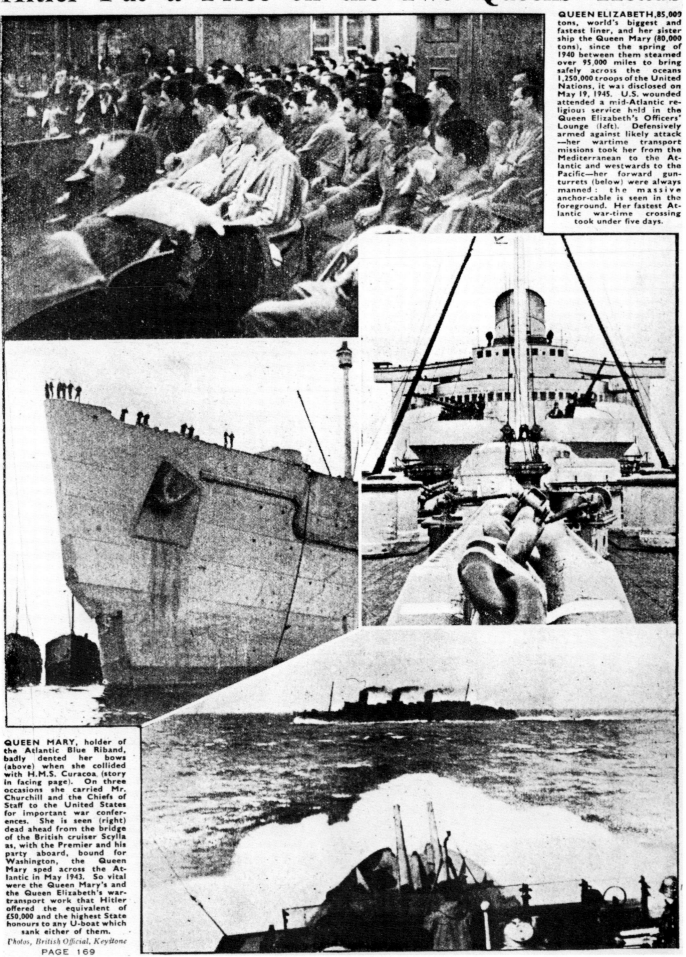

QUEEN ELIZABETH, 85,000 tons, world's biggest and fastest liner, and her sister ship the Queen Mary (80,000 tons), since the spring of 1940 between them steamed over 95,000 miles to bring safely across the oceans 1,250,000 troops of the United Nations, it was disclosed on May 19, 1945. U.S. wounded attended a mid-Atlantic religious service held in the Queen Elizabeth's Officers' Lounge (left). Defensively armed against likely attack —her wartime transport missions took her from the Mediterranean to the Atlantic and westwards to the Pacific—her forward gun-turrets (below) were always manned : the massive anchor-cable is seen in the foreground. Her fastest Atlantic war-time crossing took under five days.

QUEEN MARY, holder of the Atlantic Blue Riband, badly dented her bows (above) when she collided with H.M.S. Curacoa (story in facing page). On three occasions she carried Mr. Churchill and the Chiefs of Staff to the United States for important war conferences. She is seen (right) dead ahead from the bridge of the British cruiser Scylla as, with the Premier and his party aboard, bound for Washington, the Queen Mary sped across the Atlantic in May 1943. So vital were the Queen Mary's and the Queen Elizabeth's war-transport work that Hitler offered the equivalent of £50,000 and the highest State honours to any U-boat which sank either of them.

Photos, British Official, Keystone

PAGE 169

77

Only after the war did the Press reveal the vital importance of the Two Queens to the war effort.

78   *Queen Elizabeth* sails for New York after the end of the war with 15,000 US troops aboard.

79   In March 1942 refugees from the Japanese invasion of British colonies in the Far East arrived on the Clyde.

THE BOMBING

80   The plotting room at the Anti-Aircraft Control Headquarters of The Royal Artillery, Aitkenhead House, Glasgow.

Long before the formal outbreak of hostilities, the Luftwaffe had been preparing to wage war from the air on Britain. A major aerial reconnaissance of the country had been carried out with especial view to disabling industrial and economic targets.

Individual targets in the Clydeside area were photographed and marked in a remarkably thorough – if typically Teutonic – way (82-3).

Before the war it had always been assumed that the impact of bombing would be immediate and universally devastating. But the impact of the bomber was actually not as great as feared and the Blitz on London, which started in the late summer of 1940, became more of a war of attrition than a knockout blow. In November the Luftwaffe turned to other British cities as targets and Coventry, Liverpool, Southampton and Birmingham all suffered attack that month.

Raids on the Glasgow area were sporadic and relatively minor in effect. The first daylight raid was on July 19 1940 (86) and the first night raid was on September 18 when George Square was hit (84-5) and a lucky 500lb bomb hit the crusier HMS *Sussex* in Yorkhill Basin. The bomb went through the upper deck, the main deck, the lower deck and then exploded on the platform deck deep within the ship. Jean Brown was 17 years old and lived in the last close of Kelvinhaugh Street, opposite Queens Dock. "We had all the excitement of the night . . . the crew were thrown into the Clyde by the bomb and they were brought from the basin up to our street for clothes as most of them were naked. As the ship's magazines were full and she was all

set to sail you can imagine the state of Glasgow if the bomb had exploded! We were told to turn off water and gas and to go to Kelvingrove Park.''

But this was the sort of experience which was to become all too familiar to Clydesiders as the raids became more frequent and damaging, culminating in the great massed raids of Spring 1941. On the nights of March 13/14 and 14/15 1,083 people were killed and 1,602 seriously injured in Glasgow and Clydebank (which was devastated with only 8 houses left undamaged from a stock of more than 12,000) (92-105, 107). On the night of April 7/8 64 people died and 71 were injured (108) and in the last great raids, at the end of the first week of May, 341 died with 312 injured. This time it was the turn of Greenock and Gourock (106, 109-11).

There are many tales of the 'stiff upper lip' variety – and many of the pictures here bear ample witness as to the resilience of the Clydesider under attack – but Tom Harrisson in his study of Britons at war recounts an exchange which must have gone on many thousands of times all over the country. A Glasgow wifie has some acid words for her know-all grocer.

Grocer: *"Next week is a full moon. We shall have it again. This time they'll concentrate on Parkhead."*

Wifie: *"Has Hitler written to tell you then?"*

A map of war-damaged properties prepared by the Glasgow Master of Works and City Engineer in October 1941 survives in Strathclyde Region Archives. By this time virtually all the bombing was over and it shows the damage to have been well scattered throughout the City from Tradeston, Garscadden and Yoker (severe damage) to Dalmarnock, Hutchesonstown, Partick, Hyndland and Kelvinside. Bombs were no respecters of social class or privilege!

Clydebank had tended to become synonymous with the bombing of the Clyde region but this does not reflect an accurate picture. As a 'Secret' report on the aftermath of the raids, made by the Office of the Regional Commissioner and available at the Scottish Record Office, puts it: "The grievous nature of the damage at Clydebank . . . has tended to veil the magnitude of the attack on Glasgow." During those two nights in March Glasgow lost 647 dead with 1,680 injured and 6,835 houses damaged. More than 20,000 houses suffered minor damage. The shipyards (Yarrows and Blythswoods) at Scotstoun were badly damaged and, in contrast to Clydebank, damage was spread throughout the City. The worst incidents were at Maryhill where three tenements were destroyed (92) and 100 people were injured, and at Yarrows where 80 workers died after their shelter sustained a direct hit.

The April attacks were widespread and scattered but those of May more serious.

Greenock and Gourock were hit very hard and Edinburgh fireman Jack Grant, who was bussed in from the other side of Scotland, remembers the scene vividly: "There were no firemen about – they were all dead beat – and the mains water was off. A pump relay had been arranged from the docks and they were filling huge tanks with water in the streets. There were hundreds of hosepipes in the streets – you could hardly walk between them – and they were unattended with the nozzles jammed between stones and the water directed on the fires. I went with a warden who said, 'This is Cathcart Street and Cathcart Square. Do your firefighting as best you can.' In the whole area there was only Frankie Sweeney and me. It was like in a world of our own.

"I went into a three storey tenement in Cathcart Street to adjust the hose that was in there and suddenly the water went off. Frankie shouted to come out and I came out into the street and there was a rumble and the whole building came down."

It was thus that Jack learned that one of the first signs of a building about to come down was the water going off as the shifting structure cut the hosepipe. As the buildings cooled down they became susceptible to sudden collapse. Jack Grant remembers them falling like so many packs of cards in Cathcart Street (106). "The top flat would fall out first. Lintels and stones would fall out of the front of the building and then the whole thing went crump".

Fortunately this was the last serious air raid on the Clyde area. These raids were expensive for the Luftwaffe in terms of fuel and there were easier and more accessible targets. And just over a month later the massive Russian offensive was launched. The last air raid on Glasgow came on the night of March 23 1943. It was not a severe raid but, alas, 'Greek' Thomson's fine Queen's Park Church was destroyed. The last victim of the war from the air.

81   The Air Raid Shelter. One of Ian Fleming's series of powerful etchings.

82   Luftwaffe aerial reconnaissance photograph of Glasgow with strategic targets marked.

83   Luftwaffe aerial photograph of Govan area.

The first night air raid on Glasgow was on September 18 1940 and George Square was hit. An air raid shelter in the middle of the Square stood up to the blast of a bomb which landed beside it.

84

85   Aftermath of the September 18 air raid.

86   The first air raid on Glasgow was on July 19 1940. Damage done to a tenement in the Scotstoun district.

87   Bomb crater at Killermont Golf Course, September 1940.

88   October 1940 and severe damage was done to the Scotstoun district of Glasgow.

89   Clearing up in Scotstoun.

This house at Burnside was destroyed in the Scotstoun blitz. It was the home of Jackie Gardner, a Queens Park footballer, and he is seen searching for valuables. The censor would not allow this picture to be published at the time.

91   Damage to another house in Burnside.

92   Maryhill Blitz, March 1941. Etching by Ian Fleming.

A famous picture of the tram bombed in Nelson Street on March 17 1941.

93

94   Stonelaw School, Rutherglen, damaged in an air raid in 1941.

March 1941 and ARP workers work to free people trapped beneath debris in Peel Street, Cathcart. One man was trapped for eight days. The censor did not allow publication of this picture.

95

96   The Clydebank Blitz, March 1941.

97   The morning after the first night of the Clydebank Blitz.

98   The Clydebank Blitz

99   Cleaning up after the Clydebank Blitz.

100   Aerial view of the Radnor Park area of Clydebank, one of the worst hit areas.

101   Radnor Street, Clydebank.

102 After the Blitz.

Mary Haldane, ambulance attendant and heroine of the Clydebank Blitz. Her ambulance was blown on its side by a high explosive bomb but she carried on to rescue the occupants of another ambulance which had been completely destroyed.

Furniture salvaged from blitzed homes.

105   Burial of the unidentified dead after the Clydebank Blitz.

106   May 1941 and the turn of Greenock: severe damage in Cathcart Street.

107   After the blitzes of March 1941 many workers relied on mobile canteens which visited the bombed areas.

108   Leaving the area with what could be salvaged.

109   The front of this house at Wallace Street, Greenock, was blown away.

110   Bungalow destroyed at Glen Avenue, Gourock.

111   Bomb damage at Gourock.

112   One that got away! Unexploded land mine outside the works of Grant Cameron & Co.

113   Battered and bruised but undefeated! Survivors of the Clydeside raids.

THE CITY AT WAR

114　After the raids of March 1941 many children left urban areas around the Clyde. These children were pictured on May 1 off to the country and a new home safe from the bombs of the Luftwaffe.

In the wake of the traumas of the massed raids on Clydeside of Spring 1941 there was renewed evacuation of children to both country areas and abroad (114-18).

For the majority of people life carried on much as normal. The Clyde area was a temporary home for tens of thousands of service personnel and there were, throughout the war, distinguished visitors like Winston Churchill, General Montgomery, General de Gaulle and King George VI and Queen Elizabeth.

Many women found a liberation through the medium of the war and actively participated in the war effort through the Women's Land Army, ARP and direct employment in jobs which would have seemed scarcely suitable in peacetime (125-31).

There was great pressure to save anything and everything of no matter how little apparent value, as we can see from the graphic exhortations on the sides of the Cleansing Department trucks (134-37) with their remarkably elaborate paint jobs and blackout – defying white trims around bumpers and mudguards. All Corporation Transport vehicles had bumpers and fenders painted white, headlamps masked and interior

lighting on trams and buses was considerably reduced. The use of producer gas on bus diesel engines was fraught with difficulties and was not a success (136). By 1942, 26 buses had been converted but when government restrictions were eased in 1944 the Transport Department lost little time in converting the buses back to diesel fuel.

Women were employed as tram drivers (126) and, with the shortage of fuel, trams were left to carry most passengers. The Corporation Transport department was also responsible for the maintenance of over 13,000 Civil Defence vehicles as well as the fleet of hospital vessels used at the Tail o' The Bank anchorage. Ambulances and mobile canteens were built at the Bus Works, which had plenty of work in the aftermath of the raids. Several buses were damaged by blasting and ran with boarded up windows for a while.

There were plenty of parades, propaganda and displays (138-9) but, for most people, life carried on very much as normal. At the time, there was no great realisation of the position of the Clyde as being the vital centre of great events.

115   Evacuees, May 1941.

Bound for the country, May 1 1941.

117

For some, Canada offered a better chance for safety. This picture shows 11 year-old Thyrza McGillivray from Helensburgh at her new home with Mr & Mrs Douglas Robb of Winnipeg.

118   Children leaving for homes abroad. Gordon Scott, aged 9, from Dennistoun has his identification label checked.

119   Dockers at Yorkhill Docks enjoy a nice cup of tea from the YWCA Canteen.

Crew members of HMS *Eskimo* — survivors of Narvik — enjoy a meal in a canteen in Glasgow.

The Overseas Club, St George's Place. Picture taken just before the official opening at the beginning of April 1943.

122   A picture taken on Winston Churchill's official visit to Glasgow with President Roosevelt's special envoy, Harry Hopkins, January 17 1941.

123

124

General Montgomery's visit to Glasgow April 21 1944. At the SCWS works at Shieldhall inspecting a guard of honour provided by the Works Home Guard.

Montgomery leaves the City Chambers in George Square.

A recruiting march for the Women's Land Army passes the Cenotaph on George Square (March 1942).

Women tram drivers go on duty in Glasgow. An official picture: "Mrs Turner (centre) whose husband, a Sergeant in the RAF, is serving in West Africa."

127 Four of the 'Twentys' in happy mood after registering at a Glasgow Labour Exchange following Ernest Bevin's registration order on men over forty and young women.

128 Registering at a Glasgow Labour Exchange (April 1941). The fashions are particularly interesting.

Gas mask drill in April 1941 for the staff of a drapery firm in Sauchiehall Street.

Women at work on the LMS railway line at Cathcart.   131   Women porters on duty at the LMS College Goods Station.

132   Italians have to leave Glasgow for internment, June 1940.

133   German POWs, watched by Councillor McInnes – Glasgow Corporation sub-convenor of Housing – at work on Pollok Housing Estate making roads and sewers.

GIVE
A BOOK
GAIN
A FRIEND

THERE IS NO DOUBT THAT ANY BOOKS, WHICH CAN BE SPARED, WILL BE GREATLY APPRECIATED BY OUR MEN IN THE FIELD. I HOPE THE PRESENT DRIVE WILL SECURE AS GREAT A RESPONSE AS ITS PREDECESSORS HAVE DONE

GLASGOW'S B
21ST OCT.

The message on this Corporation of Glasgow articulated lorry is clear — "Give a book, gain a friend".

134

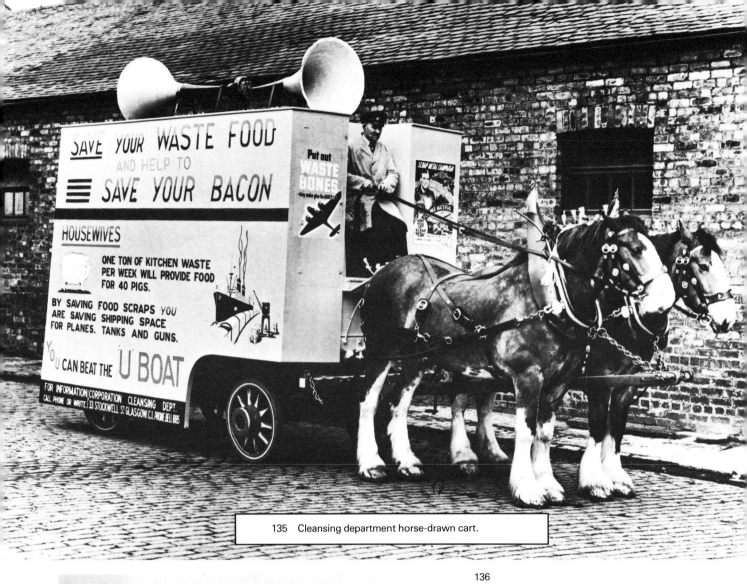

135 Cleansing department horse-drawn cart.

From May 1940 experiments with gas driven buses took place. This bus is towing a gas producer trailer unit.

"Give Rubber" was the message on this Cleansing Department lorry.

138   The National Savings travelling cinema van in George Square, September 1940.

139   'Wings for Victory' display on George Square, June 1943. Crowds lined up at 1/- a time to peep inside 'P for Peter'.

40   Queue for coke outside Tradeston Gas Works.

41   After the middle of 1941 the air raids ceased and many children came home again. These children all sport sprigs of white heather – souvenirs of their stay in the country.

INDUSTRY AT WAR

142

Manufacturing barrage balloons in the Kelvin Hall. A unique composite picture.

Glasgow and the Clyde had suffered seriously from the effects of the depression of the Thirties but the threat of war had an unmistakeably regenerative effect on the area. Preparations for war started as early as the summer of 1937. Lord Weir visited Harris Morris of Glasgow furniture manufacturers H Morris & Co in 1937. In the words of Neil Morris, his son who became managing director shortly afterwards: "We knew then it was preparation for war. Lord Weir said to my father, 'Harris, you're going to make helicopter blades'. Production of furniture stopped at our Milton Street works and a shadow factory was set up at Campsie."

H Morris & Co. made a vital contribution to the war effort manufacturing essential equipment as diverse as Lee Enfield rifles, stabilisers for barrage balloons, helicopter blades, Mosquito jettison tanks, bulkheads for motor torpedo boats, ammunition boxes and decking for landing barge pontoons. Four hundred staff worked in three shifts and every weekend. But the flying jeep never took off! (142-153)

Rolls Royce took over a 'greenfield site', to use modern parlance, at Hillington in July 1939 and within twelve months had put up an enormous complex of buildings on the 150 acre site which housed, at its peak during the War, 27,000 workers. An early employee recalled that "this achievement bordered on the miraculous – especially as the winter of that year was a severe one." There was obviously a very considerable sense of purpose, "In the early summer of 1940 everyone worked a twelve hour day, seven days a week, and every fourth week we finished at 5pm on a Saturday, but resumed as usual on the Sunday morning . . . no summer holidays were possible that year but how greatly we appreciated the long weekend from Friday evening to Tuesday morning which we were granted."

Another employee joined the company on September 4 – the day after war was declared – and was surprised on his first day at work. "I was told to go down to Block 34 and make myself generally useful.

Imagine my surprise on entering from the back door to find the front was still in the process of building!'' In an incredibly short time the factory was working on a wide range of equipment for the war effort, including the Merlin aircraft engine (154-159).

The North British Locomotive Company had been formed in 1903 from the amalgamation of three Glasgow firms (Neilson Reid, Dübs and Sharp Stewart). It was one of the greatest locomotive works in the world, made a significant contribution to the First War and was already manufacturing tanks by the time the Second War was declared. Orders for light tanks had been placed as early as 1936 and in 1940 143 were completed. These were followed by the 26-ton Matilda tank, of which 619 were built. Demand for locomotives was heavy throughout the war – which was a more mobile war than any preceding conflict – and 545 Austerity type locomotives were delivered to the order of the Ministry of Supply. As a counter to aerial cannonfire an experimental armoured engine was built

(166) to the specifications of the War Office with an ingenious method of attaching the armour so as to comply with the rigid weight limitations. In total more than 1,200 locomotives were supplied together with 1,600,000 bombs and shells, 13,000 sea mines and, by way of contrast, 800 dough mixing bowls for the Royal Navy (160-166).

As ever, the Clyde shipyards welcomed the challenge of war – especially after the enforced idleness of the Thirties. The demand both for new ships and ship repair during the War was quite insatiable as U-boat activity, especially during 1939-41, took a heavy toll of shipping (167-176).

Thirty-seven shipyards lined the river during the war years and turned out a total of 1,903 merchant and naval ships, including two battleships, four aircraft carriers and ten cruisers. Additionally, 637 vessels were converted for war and an estimated 25,000 were repaired.

143

Manufacturing Mark IV Lee Enfield Rifles at H Morris & Co.'s Milton Street works.

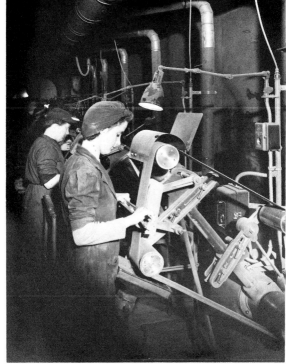

147   Machinery for sanding rifle parts.

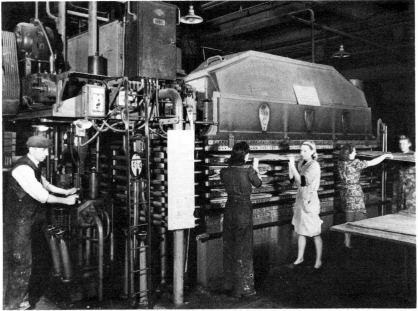

144

More than 1 million rifle parts were produced during the War on this assembly line.

145

Making decking for pontoons for landing barges.

146

Checking helicopter blades.

Irene Manning of the *New York Times* visits the factory during the period of 'lend-lease'.

149

48 Winston Churchill examines a Mark IV Lee Enfield manufactured by Morris's of Glasgow at a special presentation.

150

Moulded jettison fuel tanks.

Assembly jig for incendiary cluster containers.

151

152

53

Enter the Flying Jeep

Express Staff Reporter

LATEST wonder of the air produced in this country is the flying jeep.

A leading British aircraft constructor has successfully carried out experiments with an ordinary U.S jeep fitted with a two-bladed rotor attachment and towed by a tug plane.

A temporary fuselage is bolted on to the sides of the jeep, giving it a tail, and the rotor blades circle above the vehicle as it is pulled off the ground into the air.

Success of the experiments may lead to motor-cars being similarly adapted for peacetime travel.

Then it may be possible to clamp a fuselage and rotor on to the family car and get a tow from a friend who has an airplane.

The jeep really becomes a flying kite with rotating wings operated only by the wind pressure.

A car for Stalin

The first car from Tatra works in Czechoslovakia will be flown to Moscow and presented to Stalin.—Prague radio.

The flying jeep – one that didn't take off! Cutting from the *Daily Express* (July 7 1945).

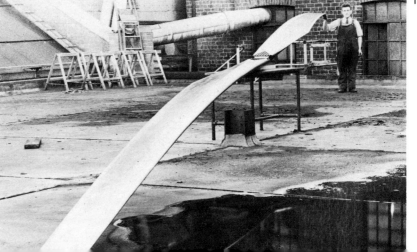

Rotor blade designed for the revolutionary flying jeep.

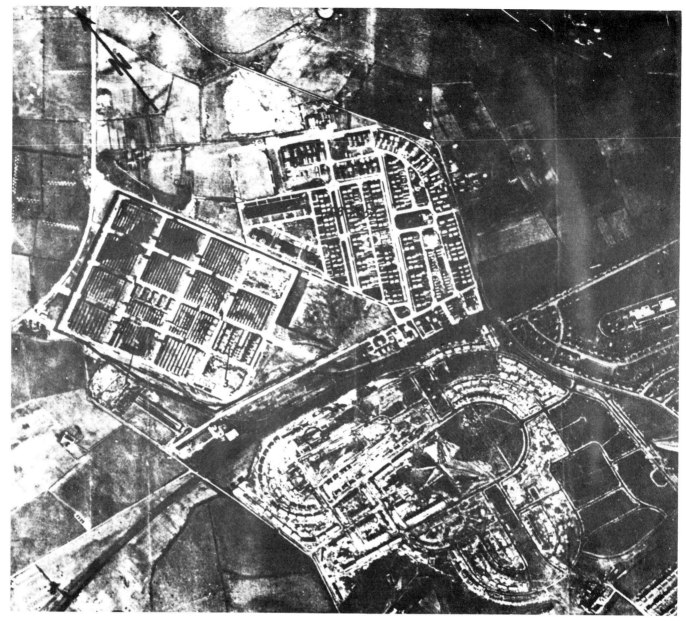

154   Luftwaffe reconnaissance photograph of the Rolls Royce Works at Hillington. Although a prime target, the factory was never hit.

155   The Hillington site in 1939.

156   The same site in the summer of 1940.

157   Women working in the foundry.

158   After hours. Foundry section entertainment.

159   Inside one of the vast factory sheds.

160   A completed tank at the Queen's Park Works of the North British Locomotive Co., 1940.

161   An Austerity locomotive for the War Department is loaded on the Clyde.

162 Working on the boiler of a 15F Class locomotive.

Tank undergoing fording test in a bath at Queen's Park Works, 1940.

164

His Majesty King George VI visited the works in 1942. Together with the Queen and senior army officers he watched a drive past of completed tanks to the testing ground (left) and it is recorded that when the Queen (below) asked one of the apprentices what he was making the youngster promptly replied, ''Time-and-a-hauf, mum!''

Austerity type locomotive for the Ministry of Supply completed 1944 at the Hydepark Works, Springburn.

Austerity type locomotive protected by special armour plating.

Taken for an official series of 'Men Behind the Ships' photographs, this is of worker J. Dover, welding on the deck of a destroyer. He played as goalkeeper for Dumbarton.

Tommy McMahon of Cathcart at his job as an oxy-acetylene cutter (from t same series). He sustained a fractured spine in the Clydebank Blitz and ret to work wearing a special spinal jacket.

Men at work on the deck superstructure of a merchant ship on the stocks. The tower of the University of Glasgow can be seen in the background.

169

170 Working on the deck superstructure of a merchant ship. Some idea of the height of the deck can be judged from the Govan Ferry crossing the Clyde in the background.

171 Adjustments to a gun in the fitting out basin.

172   Workers leaving the yard. A merchant ship on the stocks towers above (June 1945).

173   A launch in November 1942 and Sir Harry Lauder sings at the workers' request.

Lord Louis Mountbatten and his daughter Patricia at the launching of the aircraft carrier HMS *Indefatigable* in 1944.

In April 1943 Colonel Reitz – the High Commissioner for South Africa – made a two day tour of shipbuilding and naval repair yards in Scotland. Here he visits a Glasgow shipyard.

Shipyard workers of John Brown & Co. assembled at the launch of HMS *Indefatigable* by the Dowager Duchess of Milford Haven.

''It has been an eye opener . . . now I know what shipbuilding really means. You can use all the superlatives you like to tell them in South Africa how impressed I was . . .''
Colonel Reitz – High Commissioner for South Africa – addressing the Press after his tour of Clydeside shipyards, April 1943.

VICTORY

177 With D Day victory came in sight. The cruiser HMS *Glasgow* was part of a bombardment task force which attacked Cherbourg Harbour on June 25 1944. Here she can be seen under heavy fire from enemy long range and shore batteries.

With the dawn of D Day there was victory in the air and a heady mood of optimism set in. The 1944 'Glasgow Advancing' exhibition at Kelvingrove exemplified the feeling of progress and renewed confidence. As Ian Finlay put it in a book published in 1946, "The sky of Scotland was mackerelled with hope" (178-9).

The victory celebrations of the summer of 1945 were as enthusiastically embraced by Clydesiders as by all the other long suffering citizens of the country with parades, bonfires and homes and places of work decorated (180-88).

The new Labour Government received a general welcome in the west of Scotland although much good had been achieved throughout Scotland during the war years. The war had revitalised industry and from an initial figure of just over 3% of war production placed in Scotland, this had risen to 13% by 1943 involving over 50,000 workers in 370 projects in new, reopened or extended factories. The wartime Emergency Hospital Service had effectively laid the basis for the development of the National Health Service. Tom Johnston, Secretary of State for Scotland 1941-45, had laid great store by plans for peace and since 1941 regular meetings had taken place of the 'Council on Post-war Problems' which considered matters as diverse as the herring industry, hydro-electricity in the Highlands, hill sheep farming, regionalisation of water supply and unification of hospital services.

It is fortunate that the assaults, serious as they were, on Glasgow, Clydebank and Greenock had nothing of the prolonged severity of those launched on English cities. In relative terms it cannot be denied that Clydeside had been lucky and, as a result, little time had been wasted on dealing with the crises of attack and instead efforts and energies had been devoted to planning for a better future when the boys would come home and life return to normal (189-190).

178   In anticipation of victory a 'Glasgow Advancing' exhibition was held at Kelvingrove in 1944. A general view of the Transport stand.

     A view of the air transport section. An extraordinary conception of the airliner of the future! Prestwick airfield was converted into a major
179   airport during the War.

180   June 8 1945 and Victory Day. Wrens buy rosettes in Blythswood Square.

181   Open air dancing in George Square.

Victory decorations at the Trades House, Glasgow, which was one of the most gaily decorated buildings.

183   VE Day Celebrations encouraged many people to decorate their houses. This was a particularly well decorated one at Moray Drive, Clarkston.

184 Glasgow's Victory Parade. A contingent passes the saluting base in George Square. The Lord Provost, Sir Hector McNeill, is on the platform.

185

Glasgow's Victory Parade. The naval contingent in West George Street on their way to the saluting base.

186   Celebrations for everybody!

187   The Victory bonfire means fun for kids.

VJ queues in Glasgow. The war is over but the queues will continue.

188

189   A POW arrives home. Pte. W Hunter of Aitkenhead, who served in the Gordons, is driven home from Central Station by a Red Cross driver.

William McKenzie was the man who turned the lights off in Glasgow at the start of the war. Here, at the end of the war, he is pressing the button to light up the city again.

190

FACT FILE

1939

Sept	1	Evacuation of Glasgow schoolchildren begins.
Sept	3	Declaration of War. SS *Athenia* sunk in North Atlantic.
Sept	5	Survivors of SS *Athenia* landed at Greenock. First convoy leaves the Clyde. Battleship *Ramillies*, 8 destroyers and 11 transports sail for Gibraltar.
Oct	16	City of Glasgow Fighter Squadron (No. 602) shoots down the first enemy aircraft over Britain after attack on the Forth.
Dec	4	Home Fleet flagship HMS *Nelson* mined off Loch Ewe.
Dec	18	Great Canadian convoy arrives in the Clyde escorted by *Hood, Barham, Resolution, Repulse* and *Warspite*.

1940

Jan	8	Rationing of basic foodstuffs introduced.
Feb		King George and Queen Elizabeth visit Glasgow and the Clyde. U-33 fails to breach Clyde defences and is sunk by HMS *Gleaner*.
Feb	11	*Imperial Transport* torpedoed in Atlantic.
Feb	26	*Queen Elizabeth* secretly leaves the Clyde on Churchill's orders.
Apr	30	Free French destroyer *Maille Breze* explodes and sinks off Greenock.
May		Convoy to Norway sails from the Clyde.
May	26	Dunkirk evacuation begins.
June	10	Winston Churchil becomes P.M.
June	14	*Queen Mary, Aquitania, Empress of Britain* and *Empress of Canada*, escorted by battleship *Hood*, arrive in Clyde with the first contingent of Australian and New Zealand troops.
June	17	*Lancastria* sunk.
June	18	Cruiser HMS *Emerald* sails for Halifax, Nova Scotia, from the Clyde with £130m worth of gold.
July	2	*Arandora Star* torpedoed by U-47.
July	5	Gold bullion convoy sails from the Clyde. £1,800m worth of gold aboard.
July	19	Hitler offers peace terms to Britain. First daylight air raid on Glasgow.
Sept	9	London blitz begins.
Sept	18	First night air raid on Glasgow. George Square and cruiser *Sussex* at Yorkhill Docks hit.
Sept	26	Survivors of *City of Benares* arrive in Clyde.
Oct	28	*Empress of Britain* sunk 150 miles west of Irish coast.
Nov	5	Convoy HX 84 attacked in Atlantic. Tanker *San Demetrio* damaged by *Admiral Scheer*.

1941

Jan		Winston Churchill visits Glasgow together with Harry Hopkins, President Roosevelt's special envoy.
Jan	17	Dinner at North British Hotel, Glasgow, which cements British/US relations.
March	4	Lofoten Raid.
March	13/15	Massed air raids on Clydeside; Clydebank devastated.
April	7/8	Massed air raids on Clydeside.
May	5/8	Massed air raids on Clydeside; Greenock severely damaged.
May	10	Hitler's deputy, Rudolf Hess, bails out over the outskirts of Glasgow.
June	22	Germany invades Russia.
Sept	8	Stitzbergen Raid.
Sept	22	'Tank for Russia' work begins in British arms factories.
Dec	8	Britain and USA declare war on Japan.
Dec	11	USA declares war on Germany and Italy.
Dec	25	General de Gaulle visits Free French Forces in Greenock.

1942

Feb	15	Singapore falls to Japanese.
June	9	*Queen Mary* disembarks first US troops in the Clyde: 10,368 men.
June	17	Rescue ships *Perth, Zamelek, Zaafaran* and *Rathlin* for ill-fated convoy PQ 17 sail from Clyde.
June	21	Tobruk falls to Rommel.
Aug	19	Dieppe Raid by British and Canadian forces.
Oct		North African invasion fleet gathers in the Clyde.
Oct	22	First ships sail for North Africa.
Oct	2	HMS *Curaçao* run down by *Queen Mary* in the Western Approaches en route to the Clyde. 331 lost.
Nov	4	Defeat of Rommel at El Alamein.

1943

Feb	2	German surrender at Stalingrad.
March	13	Assassination attempt on Hitler fails.
March	20	Second assassination attempt on Hitler fails.
March	23	Last air raid on Glasgow.
March	27	Escort Carrier HMS *Dasher* explodes and sinks 5 miles south of the Cumbraes.
May	12	Surrender of all Axis forces in North Africa.
July	10	Allies land in Sicily.
July	24	RAF attack Hamburg with 740 planes initiating saturation bombing of German cities.
Aug	5	Churchill sails from Gourock aboard *Queen Mary* for conference with Roosevelt in Quebec City.
Sept	3	Italy surrenders.

1944

Jan	22	Allies land at Anzio.
April		General Montgomery visits Glasgow.
June	6	D-Day landings in Normandy.
Aug	25	Liberation of Paris.
Sept	5	Churchill sails from Gourock aboard *Queen Mary* for Halifax and conferences with Roosevelt.
Nov		Battleship *Vanguard* launched by Princess Elizabeth.
Dec	13	Home Guard stood down.

1945

Jan	15	First boat train to Paris since 1940 leaves Victoria Station.
March	7	US troops cross the Rhine.
April	23	Blackout restrictions lifted.
April	30	Hitler commits suicide.
May	8	Victory in Europe. German unconditional surrender. VE Day Celebrations.
May	23	Churchill resigns.
June	15	*Queen Mary* takes the first US troops (14,777 GIs) home from Gourock.
July	5	General Election campaign begins.
July	22	*Queen Mary* disembarks the last troops of the war at Gourock. Tea ration increased to 2½ oz. per person per week!
July	26	Labour Party landslide victory in General Election.
Aug	6	Atomic bomb dropped on Hiroshima.
Aug	9	Atomic bomb dropped on Nagasaki.
Aug	14	Surrender of Japan. VJ Day Celebrations.

BIBLIOGRAPHY

Local

Anderson M & Monteith J: **Greenock from Old Photographs**, Vols I & II, Greenock 1980-83.

Boyle, Gerard: **The Clydebank Blitz**, Education Resource Services, Dumbarton 1980.

Daiches, David: **Glasgow**, London 1977

Dow, James L: **Greenock**, Greenock 1975

Drummond, J D: **A River Runs to War**, London 1960

Hume & Moss: **Glasgow at War**, Nelson 1977

Hutchings & Miller: **Transatlantic Liners at War: The Story of the Queens**, Newton Abbot 1985

Kay, W (Ed.): **Odyssey: The Second Collection**, Edinburgh 1984

Macphail, I M M: **The Clydebank Blitz**, Clydebank 1974

Oakley, Charles: **The Second City**, Glasgow 1975

Wood, Ian S: **Clydebank and the Blitz**, article in *The Scotsman*, 7 March 1981

The Clydebank Blitz in Pictures, Clydebank 1980

A History of The North British Locomotive Company Ltd., Glasgow 1953

Newspaper files: *The Glasgow Herald, Evening Times, The Bulletin, Greenock Telegraph*, etc.

General

Beardmore, George: **Civilians at War**, London 1985

Calder, Angus: **The People's War**, London 1969

Churchill, Winston L S: **The Second World War**, London 1948-54

Gibson, John S: **The Thistle and the Crown: A History of the Scottish Office**, Edinburgh 1985

Hardy, A C: **Everyman's History of The Sea War**, London 1984-85

Harrisson, Tom: **Living Through the Blitz**, London 1976

Huxley, Elspeth: **Atlantic Ordeal: The Story of Mary Cornish**, London 1941

Jesse, F Tennyson: **The Saga of 'San Demetrio'**, London 1942

Johnson, B S: **The Evacuees**, London 1968

Macintyre, Donald: **The Battle of the Atlantic**, London 1961

Pelling, Henry: **Britain and The Second World War**, London 1970

Schofield, B B: **The Russian Convoys**, London 1964

Titmuss, R M: **Problems of Social Policy**, London 1950

Young, Edward: **One of Our Submarines**, London 1952

Magazines: Contemporary issues of *The War Illustrated* and *The War in Pictures*

Fiction

Monsarrat, Nicholas: **The Cruel Sea**, London 1951

Waugh, Evelyn: **Officers and Gentlemen**, London 1955

Records

Glasgow District Council, Jeffrey Room, Mitchell Libary

Scottish Record Office, Edinburgh: *Athenia* – Sinking of SS (file HH 50/6), Reports on Air Raids of 13/15 March 1941 (Files HH 50/1-4)

Strathclyde Regional Archives, Jeffrey Room, Mitchell Library.

SOURCES OF PICTURES

1 *Herald/Times* Picture Library
2 Imperial War Museum
3 Imperial War Museum
4 Imperial War Museum
5 Author's Collection
6 *Herald/Times*
7 *Herald/Times*
8 *Author's Collection*
9 *Herald/Times*
10 *Herald/Times*
11 *Herald/Times*
12 *Herald/Times*
13 *Herald/Times*
14 *Herald/Times*
15 *Herald/Times*
16 *Herald/Times*
17 *Herald/Times*
18 Museum of Transport, Glasgow
19 Author's Collection
20 Author's Collection
21 Museum of Transport
22 Museum of Transport
23 *Herald/Times*
24 *Herald/Times*
25 *Herald/Times*
26 *Herald/Times*
27 *Herald/Times*
28 Imperial War Museum
29 Imperial War Museum
30 *Herald/Times*
31 Imperial War Museum
32 *Herald/Times*
33 *Herald/Times*
34 *Herald/Times*
35 *Herald/Times*
36 A James Hall photograph courtesy
   Norman Burniston Photography,
   Greenock
37 *Herald/Times*
38 James Hall
39 James Hall
40 Press Portrait Bureau
41 Author's Collection
42 Author's Collection
43 *Herald/Times*
44 *Herald/Times*
45 *Herald/Times*
46 *Herald/Times*
47 *Herald/Times*
48 *Herald/Times*
49 *Herald/Times*
50 *Herald/Times*
51 *Herald/Times*
52 *Herald/Times*
53 *Herald/Times*
54 *Herald/Times*
55 Admiralty Photograph
56 *Herald/Times*
57 *Herald/Times*
58 Imperial War Museum
59 Author's Collection
60 Imperial War Museum
61 Imperial War Museum
62 Imperial War Museum
63 James Hall

64 James Hall
65 *Herald/Times*
66 *Herald/Times*
67 *Herald/Times*
68 *Herald/Times*
69 Strathclyde Regional Archives
70 Strathclyde Regional Archives
71 *Herald/Times*
72 *Herald/Times*
73 *Herald/Times*
74 Admiralty
75 Admiralty
76 James Hall
77 *The War Illustrated* Vol.10, p.169
78 *The War Illustrated* Vol.9, p.338
79 *Herald/Times*
80 Imperial War Museum
81 People's Palace Museum,
   Glasgow
82 Imperial War Museum
83 Imperial War Museum
84 *Herald/Times*
85 *Herald/Times*
86 *Herald/Times*
87 *Herald/Times*
88 *Herald/Times*
89 *Herald/Times*
90 *Herald/Times*
91 *Herald/Times*
92 People's Palace
93 *Herald/Times*
94 *The Bulletin*
95 *Herald/Times*
96 *Herald/Times*
97 *Herald/Times*
98 *Herald/Times*
99 *Herald/Times*
100 *Herald/Times*
101 *Herald/Times*
102 *Herald/Times*
103 *The Daily Mirror*
104 *Herald/Times*
105 *Herald/Times*
106 *The Bulletin*
107 *Herald/Times*
108 *Herald/Times*
109 *Herald/Times*
110 *Herald/Times*
111 *Herald/Times*
112 Imperial War Museum
113 *Herald/Times*
114 *Herald/Times*
115 *Herald/Times*
116 *Herald/Times*
117 Canadian Pacific Publication
    'Canada's Guests'
118 *Herald/Times*
119 *Herald/Times*
120 *Herald/Times*
121 *Herald/Times*
122 Imperial War Museum
123 Imperial War Museum
124 Imperial War Museum
125 *Herald/Times*
126 Imperial War Museum
127 *Herald/Times*

128 *Herald/Times*
129 *Herald/Times*
130 *Herald/Times*
131 *Herald/Times*
132 *Herald/Times*
133 *Herald/Times*
134 Museum of Transport
135 Museum of Transport
136 Museum of Transport
137 Museum of Transport
138 *Herald/Times*
139 *Herald/Times*
140 *Herald/Times*
141 *Herald/Times*
142 Neil Morris, H Morris & Co.
143 Neil Morris
144 Neil Morris
145 Neil Morris
146 Neil Morris
147 Neil Morris
148 Neil Morris
149 Neil Morris
150 Neil Morris
151 Neil Morris
152 Neil Morris
153 *The Daily Express*
154 Rolls Royce PLC and the Scottish
    Branch, Rolls Royce Heritage Trust
155 Rolls Royce
156 Rolls Royce
157 Rolls Royce
158 Rolls Royce
159 Rolls Royce
160 Mitchell Library, Science &
    Technology Section
161 Mitchell Library
162 Mitchell Library
163 Mitchell Library
164 *A History of the North British
    Locomotive Co. Ltd.*
165 Mitchell Library
166 Mitchell Library
167 Imperial War Museum
168 Imperial War Museum
169 Imperial War Museum
170 Imperial War Museum
171 Imperial War Museum
172 Imperial War Museum
173 Imperial War Museum
174 Imperial War Museum
175 Imperial War Museum
176 Imperial War Museum
177 Imperial War Museum
178 Museum of Transport
179 Museum of Transport
180 *Herald/Times*
181 *Herald/Times*
182 *Herald/Times*
183 *Herald/Times*
184 *Herald/Times*
185 *Herald/Times*
186 *Herald/Times*
187 *Herald/Times*
188 *Herald/Times*
189 *Herald/Times*
190 *Herald/Times*

Unnumbered photographs in the Introduction: Photograph of Ian Fleming by Paul Harris; Harry Hopkins commemorative notice courtesy the Copthorne Hotel, Glasgow; crane and bombed building logos redrawn from Polish Army Choir programme, May 1941.